D0294529

The guide for
baffled graduates

Tanya de Grunwald

summersdale

DUDE, WHERE'S MY CAREER?
Copyright © Tanya de Grunwald, 2008

Illustrations by Lee Curtis

All rights reserved.

No part of this book may be reproduced by any means, nor transmitted, nor translated into a machine language, without the written permission of the publishers.

The right of Tanya de Grunwald to be identified as the author of this work has been asserted in accordance with sections 77 and 78 of the Copyright, Designs and Patents Act 1988.

Condition of Sale
This book is sold subject to the condition that it shall not, by way of trade or otherwise, be lent, re-sold, hired out or otherwise circulated in any form of binding or cover other than that in which it is published and without a similar condition including this condition being imposed on the subsequent publisher.

Summersdale Publishers Ltd
46 West Street
Chichester
West Sussex
PO19 1RP
UK

www.summersdale.com

Printed and bound in Great Britain

ISBN 13: 978-1-84024-657-5

Tanya de Grunwald

About the author

Tanya de Grunwald is a freelance features writer from West London. She graduated from Durham University in 2000 and started writing in 2002. Tanya now works for newspapers and magazines including *Glamour*, *Grazia, eve* and *thelondonpaper*.

About The Careers Group

The Careers Group is an impartial careers advisory service that helps tens of thousands of students and graduates each year find jobs they'll love. The organisation has 40 careers advisers working in 18 higher education institutions, including University College London and Kings College London.

As well as supporting students, The Careers Group runs several hugely successful services for university leavers, including GradClub (which supports grads in their first couple of years after uni), C2 (a nationwide service offering careers advice at any stage in a graduate's career) and The Guardian London Graduate Fair from The Careers Group, which is held biannually.

Don't miss!
Your 'What next?' package of must-read info at www.careers.lon.ac.uk/dude
Your interactive 'Dude' blog at www.thecareersgroupdude.wordpress.com

Thank yous

A huge thank you to everyone who has supported and encouraged me while writing this book. In particular I'd like to thank everyone at Summersdale for your spontaneity, imagination and commitment to getting everything just right, as well as the entire team at The Careers Group for your unflinching belief that this book is needed – and for making our partnership so much fun!

I'd also like to thank my brilliant and cheerful researcher Cecily Bennett, my uber-talented illustrator Lee Curtis and all the super-wise experts who donated your time and expertise so generously, including Gael Lindenfield, Romilla Ready, Dr Claire Archdall, Alistair Leathwood at FreshMinds Talent, Mark Shulman at Cumberland Ellis, Vicki McNicol at The British Dyslexia Association and Heather Collier at The National Council for Work Experience. In addition, thank you so much to all the graduates who bravely agreed to share your stories and appear as case histories in this text. Your honesty and humour are as appreciated by me as I know they will be by the book's readers in years to come.

For your advice, encouragement and general wisdom, I'd also like to thank Linda Gray, Jo Elvin, Emma Elms, Sharon Bradley, Jackie Douglas, Daniel Crewe, David Jones, Charlie Boss, Anjali Pratap, Sara Cremer, Rachael Ashley, Corrie Jackson, Katie Masters, Claire Baylis, Marianne Macdonald, Alex Bellos, Helen Johnston, Miranda Levy, Lesley Jones, Louisa Davies, Roelof Bakker, Sarra Manning, Jo Upcraft, Kate Harrison, Paul and Shameem Stegall. I'd also like to thank my friends and family for believing in me, my flatmates for putting up with me – and my brother Max, father Alex and mother Diana for being so proud of me.

Tanya de Grunwald

And one last thank you… To the visionless publisher who sent me the world's nastiest e-mail telling me this book was a rubbish idea: your mean-spirited words inspired me more than you'll ever know!

What's in this book?

Introduction

Whoever said 'The camera never lies' had clearly never seen my graduation photo. Beaming into the July sunshine, modelling a faux fur-trimmed gown and clutching a fake plastic degree (the real thing arrived weeks later), I'm doing a pretty convincing impression of someone who's got it all worked out. But I so haven't. Behind my smile lurks a guilty secret. In three years studying Psychology at Durham University, where I attended a measly six hours of lectures a week, I had done absolutely nothing about my career. *Nada.* Zip. Zero.

Need proof? Some stats from the day I graduated:

Visits to the university careers service: 0
Careers brochures collected: 0
Careers presentations attended: 0
Potential careers being considered: 0
Jobs applied for: 0
People who thought I would ever write a book about careers: 0

I had no idea that things were about to get much, much worse. Nobody warned me that within a couple of weeks of living back at home, my confidence would evaporate and my self-esteem would nose-dive. No one told me I would spend the summer working as a very grumpy 'Office Angel', or that when autumn arrived I would still be no closer to knowing what I wanted to do with my life.

This is the book I needed then.

Part 1:

Reality bites...
or does it?

Sort fact from fiction here!

Chapter 1:
In at the deep end

Every year, thousands of graduates discover that life after graduation is a serious case of 'sink or swim'. If you're drowning, take heart. You're not the only one...

Life after university is like…

   a) a bright sunny day

or

   b) a bright sunny day when you've got the mother of all hangovers?

If you answered b), you're clutching the right book. You're one of thousands of graduates who finish uni without a clue about what they're going to do next. They say they feel overwhelmed, uninspired, depressed – or just plain baffled.

Ringing any bells?

Some of you may have made it as far as attending an employer presentation or two – but left feeling disappointed that the job didn't sound a bit more, well, *fun*. Some of you may have rocked up to a one-to-one with a university careers adviser – but walked away feeling irritated when they couldn't pull your 'dream career' out of thin air, magician-style. Others may have managed to dodge mention of the word 'career' completely, body-swerving every recruitment fair, presentation and sinister-looking leaflet that came your way. 'I'll stress about all that boring stuff after graduation' you told yourself. After all, why spoil your last year of studentdom stressing about a time you never really thought would arrive?

But Graduation Day did arrive – although it felt more like Judgement Day. And now, you're suffering the worst comedown of your life. You have little or no decent work experience under your belt, no career plans in the pipeline and your CV is shamefully bald. Good lord, what were you *doing* for the last three years? Anyone would think you'd just been partying…

To earn some cash, you're serving cappuccinos, stacking shelves or stuffing envelopes. That's if you're even out of your pyjamas and earning at all. Meanwhile, you've assured everyone it's under control. But, privately, you're bricking it. You know you need to make a plan, but haven't the foggiest idea where to start. And you'd trade anything for everyone to just stop asking.

As if that's not bad enough, perhaps you're back at home, where your parents are driving you nuts. Every family function has turned into open season for your relatives to offer streams of unsolicited advice about careers that would bore you to tears. A couple of your most organised friends are already on their first step along a glittering career path and are busy earning big bucks. Left behind, you are broke, directionless and trapped on a hamster wheel of self-loathing.

Other careers guides are written for the super-motivated graduate. In other words, the person who actually needs them the least. You know the type: while you spent your uni summers doing bar work in your local or serving strawberries at Wimbledon, they were busy beefing up their CV at an international investment bank in Berlin.

This book is different, because most graduates aren't super-sorted; they're just like you...

66 I'm still unemployed – and I was at Oxford!

It's pretty embarrassing that I still haven't found a proper job – especially since I graduated from Oxford, which is considered so prestigious. I want to get into journalism but so far I've only looked for jobs on the careers and graduates pages on the Internet, which has given me the impression that there aren't that many vacancies out there. I'm trying not to get too down about it but I can't help thinking that if I'd been more organised about the job-hunting much earlier on, the last few months could have been avoided.

Hannah Gilkes, 21
2:1, English Language and Literature, University of Oxford 99

66 There are so few jobs I actually want

Since graduating I've found it really hard to find advertised jobs that I want to apply for. I look in the paper and on the Internet and all the jobs seem to be sales-based – but I'd like to get into the business or finance sector. I'm fluent in Spanish and I have a business degree – surely that makes me a decent candidate? But I haven't had much luck yet.

Daniel Davis, 23
2:1, Modern Languages (Spanish) and Business Management,
University of Manchester

" My mum kicked my butt!

Coming home after uni was a disaster. I was unemployed for three months, getting up late, watching TV and hanging out with my friends. Eventually, my mum said, 'If you don't start looking for work, your dad and I aren't going to support you any more.' It seemed harsh at the time – but now I think it was fair enough. I knew the party was over – I was broke and all my friends had started jobs so there wasn't anyone to hang out with any more. Things improved after that. When I started job-hunting, my mum turned out to be a brilliant alarm clock. She'd march into my room and turf me out of bed – Mum doesn't stand for any nonsense. Looking back, I'm glad she gave me a hard time. It's exactly what I needed!

Roland (surname withheld)

2:2, Biology, University of Bristol

" Where are all the jobs?

When I graduated, I presumed I'd find a job immediately as a sports therapist. I also assumed it would be handsomely paid – but, frankly, now I'd be happy to settle for anything I can get! The big problem is that sports therapy jobs aren't advertised in the traditional way. It's very much about who you know, or getting a work placement and being in the right place at the right time. My mum was so proud of me for getting a first. I just want her to stay proud...

Jane Hewitt, 24

1:1, Sports Therapy, University of Bedfordshire

66 I've considered deleting my degree from my CV

I always imagined I'd come straight out of uni, get my dream job as a comedy writer and my career would take off from there. I must have been living in fantasy land to have thought I would walk out of uni and instantly become the new Ricky Gervais! I've sent my scripts and CV off to numerous prospective employers including the BBC – and been faced with stony silence. It's pretty demoralising. To make ends meet, I've been doing temporary jobs I don't care about at all. I'm more deflated with every rejection. It's got to the stage where I'm not sure there's even a point in putting my degree on my CV any more, because I don't think employers care. I'm sure they'd be more impressed if I'd already spent four years working, instead of studying. Uni didn't teach me how to get a foot in the door or cope with reality. It feels like they just spat me out and expected instant success without giving me any idea about how to actually do it.

Kenny Cavey, 22

2:1, Media Practice, University of the West of England, Bristol 99

66 I'm an Oxford grad who's temping – why can't I get motivated?

I didn't even think about jobs until I graduated. In my final year of uni I put all my energy into finishing my coursework, thinking everything else could wait. At the moment I'm temping for a bit of cash – not hugely impressive I know, when I've come from one of the country's top universities. I can't seem to get started with a proper job-hunt. On my days off I usually have a lie in, watch TV and sit around the house. I know it makes me sound lazy, but I almost feel like I'd rather do nothing than think about how I'm going to get a permanent job. Besides, when I don't know what I want to do, how am I supposed to know what to apply for?

Meggan (surname withheld), 22

2:1, Psychology and Physiology, University of Oxford

66 Employers said I needed experience

When I left uni I felt confident I'd find a job that would put my degree to good use. But I got off to a terrible start. I was swamped with 'Thanks, but no thanks' letters from design companies all saying the same thing – that I didn't have enough experience. It was so frustrating – how could I get experience if no one would give me a job?!

Harry Botterill, 23
1:1, Industrial Design and Technology, Loughborough University 99

66 I feel overwhelmed

I'd really like to get into IT or management consultancy because they link so well with my degree, but when I look at graduate websites, the sheer scale of jobs on offer seems so daunting.

Steve Meek, 23
1:1, Natural Sciences (with Physics and Maths), Durham University
MA Business Management (distinction) 99

66 No one was interested in my Cambridge degree

For the four years I was studying at Cambridge, the professors drummed into us that we were the 'crème de la crème', that the whole world was waiting for us to graduate and that employers would be beside themselves with excitement when we applied for their jobs. Realising life isn't as easy as that is a real slap in the face. I feel I've been sold an alternative view of reality – rather than the real, harsh one of unemployment and rejection.'

Demelza Bowyer, 25
2:1, Modern and Medieval Language, University of Cambridge 99

66 There's no one to ask for advice

Studying law at Cambridge was pretty high-pressure, but the stress of having to find a job after uni is just as bad. Suddenly, there is no one to tell me why I keep getting overlooked for jobs. What am I doing wrong?

Fiona Ball, 21

2:1, Law, University of Cambridge

The truth about graduate career planning

Most people plan their career in their final year, right? 'Wrong,' says Susie Goldie, Head Careers Consultancy at The Careers Group, University of London.

'If you're worried that you're the only one of all your classmates who hasn't yet "sorted out" your career, remember that this is unlikely to be the case. The truth is that many students don't use any form of careers support from their university until they're just about to graduate – or never get round to it at all. Is this because they don't need it – because they already have the perfect plan? Not from our experience. We don't just work with undergrads and recent graduates – we also work with people who left university a few years ago (in a programme called C2). What we find is that it's the people who *appeared* to have a plan all worked out when they graduated who later discover their decision isn't one they want to stick with forever, after all.

'Why does this happen? We believe it's because, unless you've had the opportunity to be exposed to experience of different jobs, predicting what sort of work you'll enjoy and what you really want out of a job is extremely tricky. That's why it can be a good idea for graduates to try out a few jobs in the first few years after university, to see what might suit them best in the long-term. There really is no need to plan your entire career the minute you graduate – in fact, it's pretty much impossible.'

66 Why did I leave it so late?

When I graduated it suddenly hit me – I was jobless, without a plan. I regret not finding work experience while I was studying because it seems the people that did landed jobs straight away. There are so many graduates now that it's not just about my degree any more but about having something extra that makes me stand out from everyone else. But how?

Bola Giwe, 22

2:1, Politics and Business, University of Greenwich 99

66 Job-hunting is exhausting

I never expected job-hunting to be so time-consuming and so draining. My friends and I are only just realising how lazy we were at uni! The only thing that's reassuring is knowing that so many of us are in the same boat.

Sophie Goddard, 23

2:1, English Literature with Language, University of Brighton 99

66 I'm struggling to get noticed

I want to start off as a junior graphic designer but it isn't going well. Employers want people with experience – but I can't get experience if I can't get a job! I've sent off about 30 portfolios, and I usually wait a week before chasing up an application, but it's usually the same brush-off: 'Oh, I haven't seen it yet' or 'It must be with my assistant.' It's so frustrating, when I know I've got lots to offer. Sometimes I wonder if I should give up and get a normal job, like working in a call centre or something. But I have a lot of confidence in what I can do. I know I'm worth more than the treatment I'm getting. I've started applying to companies that haven't even advertised available jobs – and I'm starting to have more luck that way. I'm hopeful that I'll get there in the end. I just didn't expect it to take this long.

Rian Howells, 22

2:1, Graphic Design, University of the West of England, Bristol

The graduation blues

Why do so many of us feel so rubbish when we graduate? Dr Claire Archdall, psychiatrist at Bristol Royal Infirmary, explains:

'Finishing university is billed as being a really exciting time, but it's just as common for graduates to feel lost, frightened, anxious or overwhelmed. Depending on your circumstances, this might be the first time you've had no structure or definitive purpose to your life. Until now, life has been spent working towards goals set by different figures of authority. Suddenly, graduates are told to create their own goals, which can be very daunting.

'Throw in financial worries, the seemingly endless number of options available (including travelling or further study), being separated from friends or partners, plus huge expectations from friends and family and it's no wonder this stage of life can feel so uncomfortable for so many graduates. They often feel that the calibre of their educational opportunities and achievements only add to the pressure to produce spectacular results immediately. Failure to do so can lead to a loss of confidence which can actually make it harder to focus on pursuing future plans and goals.

'Graduating can also trigger what psychologists call an "identity crisis". The role of "student" has gone and there may be no natural replacement, which means graduates are unsure of what their role in society is.

'For most graduates, all these feelings dissipate once they find a job and their self-esteem begins to rise. But until that happens it's important graduates keep an eye on how they're feeling. Suffering the "graduation blues" can increase your risk of developing a depressive illness.'

Worried your graduation blues have become something more serious? For information on what to do if you think you may be suffering from depression, turn to Chapter 10: Rescue Remedies.

66 I know where I want to be – but I can't see a way in

I thought I knew I wanted to get into advertising, but when I finished uni, it didn't seem that there were enough jobs available. It would really help if there was an advertising qualification I could get, but there isn't one. Without that structure, I'm struggling to find a way to get a foot in the door. I'm quite jealous of friends who studied medicine, architecture or law, because as soon as they finish uni they just become doctors, architects and lawyers. But what happens to the rest of us?

Jan Ilett, 22

2:1, Language, Literacy and Communications, University of Manchester 99

66 Was my degree a waste of time?

I sometimes wonder whether I should have bothered with university at all. My parents are supportive but I feel like a big disappointment to them both. My dad never went to uni and was so proud when I got in. I dread family parties because everyone always asks what I'm doing with my life and I feel they're all really disappointed that I have a degree but am not doing something better for a living. I try not to let it get to me but at the moment I'm feeling pretty low – like I'm losing my way. Other days I just feel really angry. I don't feel I deserve to be in this situation – not after all the effort I've put in.'

Jennifer Needham, 24

2:1, Fashion and Brand Promotion, University of Central Lancashire 99

66 I still feel like a student – but now I'm called 'unemployed'

The thought of having a full-time job is almost as daunting to me as the thought that I still have to find one. I still feel like a student so it's weird thinking that I'm entering this completely adult world of deadlines and professional responsibility. I can't help but feel nostalgic about uni days, where I could get out of bed in the afternoon and didn't have much responsibility, short of getting to lectures and handing assignments in on time. But it looks like those days are well and truly over!

Olivia Marks, 21

2:1, Cultural Studies, University of Leeds

How has it come to this? Why is it that year after year thousands of graduates finish university without any idea of what to do next? How do they get themselves into such a pickle?

Step one: deny, deny, deny

In your final year, you adopt the 'ostrich strategy' towards your future. Careers advisers nationwide confirm that year in, year out, students leave it until the summer term of their final year to haul themselves in to 'have a chat' with them – and that's the organised ones. Plenty of you never show up at all. This vast 'lost' group just refuse to engage in discussion about jobs and careers – you don't even want to *think* about what will happen after graduation. Perhaps if you just ignore it, it'll all go away...?

Step two: reverse

Going home to live with your folks is a serious downer after graduation. After three years living away from home, feeling confident and independent, moving back in with your parents was never going to be a great boost, was it? Suddenly, you're back with your school friends, hanging out at your old local. It can feel as if your university years never happened. Real masochists go even more retro by returning to their depressing summer job, too.

Step three: lose confidence

Your va-va-voom vanishes. You leave uni feeling invincible – but that confidence soon evaporates when you're no longer around people who make you feel good about yourself. Now you can't leave the house without the sense that the whole world knows what a pathetic, over-educated, jobless loser you are. When you're in this emotional state, how are you supposed to put your best foot forward in a job interview?

Step four: fear the future

Good old-fashioned terror can be crippling for graduates. With life after university billed as the time to *get serious*, it's no wonder it feels like the end of all fun. You're dreading being sucked into a grown-up life you don't want. Suddenly, your world feels vast and unfamiliar. But check whether your fears are based on fact, rather than stereotypes and misconceptions...

Luckily, there is help at hand – in the next nine chapters of this book.

In Chapter 2…

Discover why things aren't nearly as bleak as they seem – honest!

Chapter 2:
Myth-busting

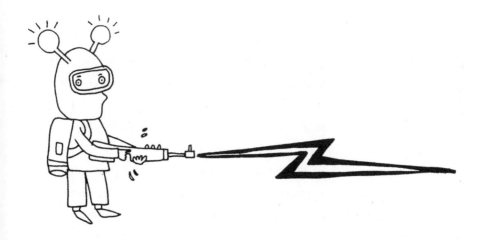

Don't believe everything you hear – there's a lot of rubbish being talked out there. Get smart by zapping those tall tales now...

I met hundreds of recent graduates when researching for this book. I asked about your plans and the reasons for those plans. I asked about your fears and the thinking behind those fears. And the more of you I spoke to, the clearer it became that there are a huge number of myths, fibs and half-truths sloshing about out there.

Stranger still, I discovered that they're exactly the same myths that were knocking about when I graduated in 2000. (I'm almost disappointed that no one has had the imagination to fabricate any fresh rubbish since then, but still…) This seemed pretty weird to me, given there's so much *good* information about out there now. Until I realised that's precisely the problem: there's too much information. Employers and careers services bombard graduates with books, brochures, leaflets and website links. But instead of inspiring you, they leave you feeling more baffled than ever. Everybody has their own opinion. Everybody has different advice (and different reasons for giving you that advice – more of which later). Which is right?

When your head is spinning, it's all too easy to mistake the myths that come your way as cold, hard fact – not realising that they are in fact the monstrous love children of half-baked opinion and Chinese whispers. That's right: long before these scare-stories reached your ears, they were passed among hundreds, maybe thousands, of people. The facts are twisted, moulded and mangled. They are repeated endlessly until they become 'fact' – or at least, received wisdom.

The theme of these myths tends to be how gruelling life is after graduation. The truth is that it needn't be – once you've sorted the facts from the fiction and calmed yourself down with a nice mug of tea. But when you're swamped by negative nonsense like this, it's easy to miss the good stuff that would actually make your life easier. So you just press on, flailing around, hoping that some employer, somewhere, will come to your rescue and throw you a life raft – in the form of a job you don't really want.

I think you can do better than that – and discovering the truth will help clarify the task ahead. In this chapter, you'll come eyeball-to-eyeball with ten of the scariest myths out there. Be brave, and I'll show you why they're no more real than ten ghost stories. Not only that, but I think you'll find it encouraging. The truth is far, far friendlier than the myth. Trust me – there is no bad news!

Why are these myths so dangerous?

Susie Goldie, Head Careers Consultancy at The Careers Group, explains…

'Treating the many graduation myths as fact can be destructive for two reasons. First, they can distort your view of the task ahead. Graduates might start to believe they need to choose a career for life right now, or that they can't change jobs if their first plan doesn't work out. If they're not careful, they can find themselves working to achieve a list of unnecessarily unrealistic and inflexible goals.

'Second, believing the bad news (especially without realising the good news) can have an enormous impact on how graduates feel – which can impair their ability to job-hunt effectively. It's hardly surprising – thinking you need to commit to the next job you take for the next forty years would trigger paralysis in the best of us.

'It's crucial to find out the facts before you go any further, so you don't make decisions based on hearsay. Whatever you do next should be a considered move, not a stab in the dark. This chapter should really help you get a few things straight.'

> ## Myth: 'Most people have their career planned out by the time they graduate – or soon afterwards'

Perhaps you think...

You're one of a tiny minority of graduates who haven't yet decided what to do with the next 40 years of their working lives. Everyone else has their entire career mapped out ahead of them. All they have to do now is get on with it. You need to do the same – sharpish.

Reality check:

Every year, a king-size slice of the student body graduates without so much as an inkling about what they're going to do next – and most go on to live happy, successful lives. Honest. Our experts at The Careers Group can testify that very few 21-year-olds know how they're going to spend their entire working lives. And even if some think they do, many of them will change their minds later.

Before I continue, I'm going to make a statement that might seem controversial, given the title of this book: I have a real problem with the word 'career'. I think, all too often, the way that it's used is enormously misleading, supremely unhelpful and totally out of date. I'll explain...

Throughout your time at school and university you are encouraged to think of your 'career' as something you can plot in advance. Understandably, you start to assume it's possible to sketch out your future employment from the age of 21 to your mid-60s.

But, as you're starting to discover, that's not exactly the way it works for everybody – for most of us, in fact. For the majority of people, the series of jobs we take during our working years only becomes a true 'career' when we look back on it. You can't really plan a career at all – because it doesn't actually exist until you've done it. For now, it's simply the future.

The whole point of the future is that you don't know what it's going to be like until you get there. Just as you don't yet know where you'll be living, whether you'll be married, have children, be rich or poor, bald or fat – nor can you possibly plan your future jobs in advance. Not only will your priorities shift as time goes on, leading you to make all sorts of decisions you probably never imagined, but the world will change too – and that affects the job market in ways you can never predict. Do you think students who graduated in the early 1990s had any idea how many of them would be doing jobs involving something called the 'World Wide Web'?

OK, I know the future can seem a bit daunting – particularly when you've become so used to having your life clearly mapped out for you throughout your education. But all that's required is a shift in your thinking.

Instead of planning everything and then getting on with it, you're going to have to get used to feeling your way, making decisions as you go along. Through trial and error, you'll discover what's working for you and what isn't. Anything can – and will – happen. Only one thing is certain: you'll have to keep changing the plan.

Know lots of people with clear 'careers'?

Have you met lots of people who have worked their way up through a series of jobs, with one leading logically onto the next? It might sound like a planned 'career', but listen closer and you'll hear that they're telling their story with hindsight. Knowing how things turned out distorts the past. Their haphazard decisions become genius, insightful and focussed 'career moves'. But don't be fooled. Just like everyone – including you – they found their way as they went along. It may seem that the person you're talking to had a grand plan all along, but really they could have taken an infinite number of paths to all sorts of destinations. You're only hearing about one.

66 Just get started!

I didn't know what I wanted to do as a career so decided to put off my job-hunt and work as a labourer, renovating houses. It wasn't bad, but I soon realised that I really did want to do something more challenging – even if it wasn't my 'dream career' for life. I started using my evenings to job-hunt and landed a job with Boots, where I'm now a junior buyer. Will I be in this job forever? Who knows? What I do know is that I'm learning far more and having a lot more fun than I did renovating houses! The people are great and the job has really boosted my confidence...

James Brewer, 24
2:1, International Business Studies, Sheffield Hallam University

66 I graduated – and panicked!

When I graduated, I felt this huge pressure to decide immediately what to do with the rest of my life. My degree was a mixture of languages and politics so everyone kept suggesting becoming an interpreter or a teacher – but neither of those options appealed to me. So I panicked. I was so desperate to find an alternative that I applied for anything and everything, without thinking about what job I might actually enjoy, or be any good at. It was only when I was offered a job in finance that I really didn't want that I thought, 'Oh my god, what am I doing?!' Since then, I've calmed down about job-hunting – and my head feels much clearer. Looking back, I realise I was trying to take five steps instead of one. I still don't know exactly what I want to do with my life. But I realised it doesn't matter. My first step is just to find a job I enjoy for a bit. I'll figure out the rest as I go along.

Julia Edwards, 22

2:1, European Studies, Durham University

66 I'm leaving my options open

I've been working in Denmark for five months as a junior designer for Lego. When people ask when I'll be coming home, I tell them I honestly don't know. The job and training are brilliant, my prospects for promotion look promising and my colleagues are fun to work with. I've realised I don't need to map out my entire future right now. At the moment, I'm just making the most of the amazing opportunity I've been given.

Harry Botterill, 23

1:1, Industrial Design and Technology, Loughborough University

TOP TIP

Don't compare yourself to your high-flying friends. Make your own choices when you're ready. Remember the tortoise and the hare?

It's now entirely acceptable to chop and change jobs throughout your career. Why? Well, for starters, more and more employees are claiming their right to have a job that gives them a sense of personal satisfaction. They may have started their career as, say, a solicitor, but if they decide they'd prefer to become a primary school teacher (and are prepared to accept a drop in salary in exchange for greater enjoyment at work), they do just that. They're simply adjusting their job in line with their priorities in life.

Second, employers have wised up to the fact that people who have gained experience in one industry can actually bring even more to another industry. For example, newspaper editors sometimes become successful celebrity PRs, because they have experience on 'the other side of the fence'. Smart employers know that hiring a team from a range of professional backgrounds means gaining a range of different perspectives.

And third, it's a fact of life that there is less job security now than in your parents' day. When companies merge or sell off departments, you're likely to find some restructuring as staff are rearranged to meet the demands of the new set-up. Often, this means redundancies (as companies are answerable to their shareholders and profit is everything). With this prospect always looming, employers can no longer pledge guaranteed structured career progression to their staff.

Think this sounds like bad news? Not necessarily. Look at it another way; if your employer isn't loyal to you, you don't have to be loyal to them. Kind of sad? Maybe, but it's also liberating, because the lack of commitment on both sides brings a sense of freedom which continues throughout your working life. Employers accept that their employees always have an eye out for better opportunities somewhere else. People don't sit and wait for promotion any more. If you suspect you'd be better valued by a different employer, then approaching your company's biggest rival for a job isn't seen as back-stabbing – it's considered shrewd. However well you get on with your boss on a personal level, there's always an underlying assumption that it's every man for himself...

The good news:

You don't need to pick your career at all – and anyone who says they've chosen theirs for life is talking nonsense (probably). If you don't know exactly what you want to do, you don't need to worry. You can work it out as you go along. At this stage, all you need is a bit of direction and to find a cracking first job that will start you off on your journey. The rest of this book is designed to help you do just that.

Did you know...?

Only 24 per cent of the attendees at a recent recruitment fair organised by The Careers Group were undergraduates. That's right – over three-quarters of those who turned up had already graduated, and were still seeking inspiration. And they weren't just the dummies, either. Seventy-one per cent of those who were there had a 2:1 or above.

Myth: 'If I try a job and hate it, I'll get stuck for the rest of my life.'

Perhaps you think...

Your first job is a big commitment – so you need to think carefully before jumping in with both feet. If it turns out to be a stinker (bad people, wrong role, or the industry isn't what you hoped), then that's tough luck; you're stuck with it. Other employers won't look at people who have worked at a job for less than a year. They just label you a 'job hopper' and move on to the next CV in the pile.

Jobs for life – dead and buried!

Your parents may have picked one vocation and stuck with it, but don't be misled. Things have changed a fair bit since then. Nowadays, it's very unusual for people to stick with one role or industry for life. Today, many professionals (in most industries) adopt more of a 'portfolio career' approach, collecting transferable skills and experience and switching roles and industries several times in a lifetime.

Reality check:

You have more flexibility than you think. As I said earlier, if you don't graduate with a burning desire to pursue a particular job, the best thing to do is to shift your mindset to a 'trial and error' mentality, whereby you make informed choices and see how you get on. However, this approach is not without risk: you might make an 'error' and take a job that you end up not liking quite as much as you thought you would. Of course, there are steps you can take to minimise the risk of this happening (like matching your personality to the role, see Part 2, The three-day-plan).

I'm not going to lie, though – it does happen. There are all sorts of reasons why your first job might not work out the way you (and your employer) had hoped. The role might not be what you expected, the people might not be very nice, you might not find the work as interesting as you thought... It isn't ideal – but it isn't a disaster either.

Nor is it something that only happens to graduates. As any recruiter will testify, people continue to make 'wrong turns' throughout their career, snapping up all sorts of jobs that seem like a good idea, but turn out not to be. For employees – and employers, too – this is simply a fact of life. Not everybody who is hired will take to the job or the company like a duck to water.

The downer, of course, is that you'll have to go back to the drawing board and apply for a new job – which is boring. And yes, in future interviews, you'll probably have to explain why things 'didn't work out' at your last role. But does it mean you'll never work again? No. Will you get a reputation as a serial job hopper? No.

Having said that, if you have five months on your CV as a marketing assistant, then three months as a lion tamer, another six months in hotel management before you decide you want to get into corporate finance then yes, potential employers will start to wonder what's going on. But there's a big difference between taking one job that doesn't work out, and taking three or four in a row. Most employers will cut you some slack. If you can give sensible reasons why you took your duff job in the first place, The Careers Group say, nine times out of ten recruiters are likely to be understanding. They know that lots of grads take a while to find their feet after university, so most will give you something of a 'grace period' while you get your act together. They know that when it comes to navigating your future, a few wrong turns and scenic detours are to be expected.

And there's more good news: some might even see your 'error' as a good thing. Seriously! The Careers Group say that an increasing number of employers are now starting to see grads with a bit of experience elsewhere as a serious asset. The advantage for them is these graduates are not totally 'green' (i.e. fresh out of uni). In other words, by the time you come to them, you'll have a bit more knowledge and experience under your belt (and therefore have more sophisticated judgement). As a bonus, you'll already have made many of your inevitable early mistakes while someone else was paying your salary.

The scenic route to success

Did you know that…

* in the early 1980s, actor Steve Buscemi spent four years working as a New York firefighter?
* when comic Jimmy Carr graduated from the University of Cambridge, he spent almost two years as a marketing executive for Shell?
* fashion designer Ralph Lauren served in the United States Army from 1962 to 1964?
* after she graduated from Oxford, and before she launched travel website lastminute.com, Martha Lane-Fox worked for business strategy consultants Spectrum for a year?
* in the early 1990s, Jo Elvin, now editor of *Glamour* magazine, spent six months as a publicist on *Neighbours*?
* former Prime Minister Margaret Thatcher worked as a research chemist for a plastics engineering company?
* writer Franz Kafka spent nearly a year working for an Italian insurance company?
* before he became an author, Charles Dickens was a law clerk, then a court stenographer?
* Karl Marx – philosopher, political economist and revolutionary – once worked as a correspondent for the *New York Herald Tribune*?
* ex-tabloid editor Piers Morgan once worked for insurers Lloyds of London?
* smoothie kings Richard Reed, Adam Balon and Jon Wright met at Cambridge University but spent four years working in advertising and management consultancy before launching Innocent Drinks together?

Other employers deliberately rotate graduates around different departments during their first year in a job to give them as broad a knowledge base as possible and allow them to see their roles in a wider context. In other words, moving around a bit gives employees a better perspective.

The good news:

If taking a first job that turns out to be wrong for you is your idea of a 'worst case scenario', then it really isn't that bad. You'll still have learnt more about what you do and don't want than you would from staying in that mind-numbing temp job or your old summer job. However pear-shaped a job goes – if the role turns out to be the opposite of what they told you, or your boss morphs into Satan, for example – you'll still be more employable than you were before you took the job. Why? Because you'll have more experience than you did when you started. Yes, even if it was a bad experience.

Taking a first job that turns out to be a total stinker really isn't the worst case scenario. The worst case scenario is staying in that job.

Worried you'll be too scared to leave a duff job?

Many grads fear feeling boxed in, or getting too comfy in a job that's going nowhere. If you really hate a job, or if staying there is making you hate yourself, just remember: however hemmed in you feel, you can always leave. Yes, it means having the awkward 'Guess what? I'm leaving' chat with your boss. And yes, it might mean handing back your starting bonus. But it's your life – and you're in charge. If you want to leave, do it. On to pastures new!

> **Myth: 'Once you're on a graduate scheme, the rest of your life is sorted.'**

Perhaps you think...

Graduate training programmes are the best and easiest way to fast-track career success. The interviews are tough because they only take the best of the best – but once you're in they treat you like royalty and take care of the rest of your career. Plus, you get a hefty starting bonus and a nice fat salary. If you can't get accepted on to a graduate training scheme, you'll have to start at the very bottom, with all the people without degrees. In the long term, you'll be years behind your peers.

Reality check:

As tempting as they may seem, graduate schemes aren't always the answer to your prayers. They don't suit everybody.

Of course, schemes *can* be a good way to get cracking and gain some solid experience. For some grads, they're perfect. When they sign the contract, they understand exactly what the job involves and know that it's likely to be work they'll enjoy. For them, the scheme gives them the structure and focus they need – and many end up staying in that industry for a good many years to come, doing well for themselves and enjoying the work. The starting bonus or 'golden handshake' is a very nice extra.

Others will find that graduate training schemes just don't quite work for them. There's something a bit 'one size fits all' about them. Whilst some find they fit like a glove, others will find them an uncomfortable squeeze.

Before you accept a job on a scheme, consider why you're so keen to sign up. What makes this option seem so attractive? Is it just because it's structured? After school and uni, it's natural to want to find a new place to belong, where someone else is going to do all the thinking and organising for you and all you have to do is turn up.

If you're having any doubts before you accept a position, it's worth checking the small print in your contract to see how much flexibility your new employer is prepared to give you if things don't go to plan and you decide to leave before the end of the scheme. Some companies ask you to hand back some of your starting bonus if you quit before a fixed period of time, which can be a very a nasty surprise. Particularly if you've already spent it – gulp...

Other graduates go into schemes fully prepared to fulfil their obligations, but harbouring a secret plan to 'cheat the system' by quitting immediately afterwards – once they've saved a heap of cash – to pursue their true passion, usually a riskier or poorer-paid profession. If this is you, then watch your step. Many people find it difficult to follow through with the final part of the plan. After investing several years of their life and working hard to gain the respect of others, quitting suddenly seems downright silly. The moment to take a risk and go for what you really wanted has passed. Three years on, the chances you'll actually leave your well-paid job as a management consultant to go and become a field archaeologist are slim.

What's the answer? Well, if you're unsure, don't get rushed into committing to a job you might regret. Instead, buy time. If you want a permanent job but fear being 'locked in' with a huge corporation, it's worth investigating smaller companies, who are less likely to ask you to commit to three years or to use a 'golden handshake' starting bonus to entice you to do so. Just because they aren't offering a graduate 'fast-track' scheme doesn't mean they won't take your degree seriously or offer a salary that reflects your academic achievements. Find a nice company with great people, and take a job with them. That way, you can get on with gaining some experience, but still keep your options open. What you learn in that job will be useful experience, whether you stay in that line of work or not. A job like this probably won't be as handsomely paid as one with a big corporation, but if you decide you don't like it, you can simply leave.

Alternatively, if you'd prefer not to commit to a permanent job at all, why not look into an internship or a job with a short-term contract? A company might be looking to hire someone to cover an existing employee's maternity leave, or they might just need an extra pair of hands during a particular period – like the summer, when lots of people take holiday, or during the run-up to Christmas, when many businesses are particularly busy. Internships and short-term contracts can be a fantastic way to gain a bit of experience without committing yourself to a role or company long-term. Who knows, if you find that you like them and they like you, they might even ask you to stay on. (For more information on work experience, see Chapter 8.)

The good news:

Going it alone gives you more options. If you've been restricting your job search to companies that offer swanky fast-track graduate placements, you've been missing out on a host of other companies you might well find more inspiring (and more fun). Their starting salaries might not be quite as impressive, but they should be fair. And they won't try and sign you up for life to a job you aren't even sure you want.

Myth: 'It's unrealistic to expect to love your job.'

Perhaps you think...

University is fun – the working world sucks. It's hard work, it's boring and it's for the rest of your life. The party is officially over.

Reality check:

Choose the right job and work can actually be quite fun. No, seriously! There are zillions of great companies out there, working on new, exciting and challenging projects. Take a job with one of them and you can work for a brilliant, inspiring boss and meet smart, feisty colleagues who make you laugh in meetings and will gossip with you at lunchtime. Of course, you won't love your job all day, every day, but it's absolutely realistic to aim to love large chunks of it – most days.

It's easy to see why the myth that all work is tedious, depressing and horrible is so readily swallowed. 'Work' as opposed to 'play' is suffering a serious image crisis. The word alone conjures images of dreary, grey offices, stuffed with workers hemmed in like battery hens. Where 'bosses' are mean and miserable and 'colleagues' are bored and unmotivated.

This myth is pedalled by mediocre people who are too scared – or can't be bothered – to leave their job and do something more challenging. They want everyone to be as miserable as they are. But this is not how it has to be for you. Aim higher.

The good news:

You don't have to spend the next 40 years of your life doing a job that leaves you feeling like you've sold your soul. You can choose to spend it doing all sorts of things you enjoy, with people who inspire you and make you laugh.

Want to know how to find a job you'll enjoy? Read The three-day plan in Part 2.

Myth: 'Companies that don't advertise don't have any vacancies.'

Perhaps you think...

All the interesting jobs have already been taken – that's why you never see them advertised. All jobs have to be advertised, it's the law.

Reality check:

No one knows what percentage of vacancies is advertised; it's an impossible statistic to find because when employers fill a role without advertising they have no reason to register this fact anywhere. What is known is that it isn't anywhere close to 100 per cent. Some sources even put it as low as 20 per cent.

I know – it seems weird, doesn't it? After all, if recruiters don't *tell* people there's a job going, how on earth can they ever hope to find good candidates? Are they completely stupid? Actually, no – there are very good reasons why some employers never advertise. And no, it isn't against the law.

For starters, advertising vacancies is really expensive for companies. You've probably never given it much thought, but recruiters have to pay a lot of money to advertise their vacancies – particularly in national newspapers. As a result, job ads you see contain clues about how much money the employer is prepared to spend on finding good candidates. As a general rule, the more eye-catching the ad, the more expensive it is. Big ads cost more than small ones, colour is pricier than black and white, and space near the front of the jobs section is more expensive than space at the back. And how fancy is the ad? If it looks professionally designed, the recruiter almost certainly hired a professional firm to do it for them, bumping up their costs further still.

Newspapers aren't the only way recruiters try to reach graduates. Did you ever pick up any of those freebie graduate magazines, leaflets or books? If you did, you probably noticed they too contain recruitment advertising. (Incidentally, that's where the money comes from to get these 'free' materials produced). Again, it's no coincidence that these pages are bought by the big corporations and feature high-quality advertising. It's these companies that have the budget to hire the best advertising professionals to design them.

Now think back to the careers presentations and recruitment fairs you went to, or saw advertised. Do you remember seeing any small companies there? Nope, didn't think so. Again, buying time and space at these events is seriously pricey – and only the biggest companies can afford to do it. For smaller companies, it isn't really worthwhile. They might only hire one or two graduates a year, whereas the big companies might hire hundreds. For small companies, the maths of advertising vacancies just doesn't add up.

That the bigger companies – with deeper pockets – dominate the advertising space is all perfectly legal, of course; that's just the way things are. It's not right or wrong – but you should be aware of how it works.

Why? Because the type of advertising you see will seriously skew your impression of the current job market. Just because you don't see vacancies for small or medium-sized companies, it doesn't mean there aren't vacancies at those companies. All it means is that it doesn't make financial sense for those companies to advertise vacancies by traditional means. Instead, these companies might advertise on their own website – which is free. They might ask around – also free, although sometimes existing employees receive a reward for bringing a fantastic friend to join the company. Or, they might just hope that the best candidates will have the nous to approach them, regardless of whether they've seen a job advertised. For more on this, see the section on the 'If you don't ask' approach in Chapter 6.

Second, advertising vacancies isn't the best way to find top-quality candidates. As any recruiter will tell you, advertising a job doesn't guarantee hundreds of brilliant candidates will apply. Employers frequently complain that they are inundated with too many applications – most of which are complete dross. The people who apply aren't always the people the recruiter wants.

Take the media industry, for example. Advertising a junior TV, magazine or film job will see the recruiters swamped with literally hundreds of candidates. For these employers, this is not helpful. Sifting through the applications is hugely time-consuming, and all the candidates will have a similar, fairly low, level of experience. To reduce the numbers, media recruiters need to use an extra screening tool, something that will save time and effort. They need a personal recommendation. So they shout, 'Have we had any really good work experience people in, lately? Get them in for an interview!'

Third, some companies don't need to advertise. Ever wondered why you rarely see ads for smart, forward-thinking, popular brands? It's simply because they don't need to advertise. After all, why spend money on

Isn't it illegal not to advertise jobs?

Not exactly, says Mark Shulman, partner at city law firm Cumberland Ellis...

'It's a common misconception that it's a legal requirement for employers to advertise every vacancy. Strictly speaking, most organisations are not legally obliged to advertise a vacancy. Indeed, because advertising externally is a costly business, many companies prefer to promote existing employees into vacant roles or even ask for recommendations from contacts, rather than going to the expense of finding new people from outside the organisation.

'A lot of companies, particularly large ones, do advertise most vacancies, and in a variety of media, as this exposes them to a greater pool of talent and it protects them from accusations that they are not abiding by their legal responsibility to not discriminate during their recruitment processes.

'There is good news if you are looking for a job working for a public body – say, a council, education authority, or the NHS – as you will find that virtually all of their jobs are advertised widely. They do this as they have a duty under the law to promote diversity and equal opportunities through their recruitment policies. Therefore, public bodies generally advertise vacancies as broadly as possible in order to prevent legal claims against them for discrimination.

'Furthermore, councils have an extra legal responsibility with regards to their jobs, to try and reach as broad an audience as possible to ensure that every paid position is filled purely on merit – as opposed to candidates being advantaged by opportunity or favouritism.'

recruitment advertising when excellent candidates come to them? Why spend hours sifting through applications when candidates pre-select themselves, simply by having the initiative to apply speculatively, i.e. by sending in their CV for a job or work experience, regardless of having seen an ad for it. In doing this, these candidates have already proven they're smart enough to realise that not all jobs are advertised, and they're keen enough to apply on the off-chance that something might be available.

The good news:

Whichever industry you're interested in, there are masses more jobs out there than it first appears. If you've ever scrolled through lists of dull-sounding vacancies on job websites and had that nagging feeling you were looking in the wrong place, you might well have been right. If you've only been looking at the advertised jobs, you've only scratched the surface. Dig deeper and you might well find lots more interesting jobs.

> ## Myth: 'Holiday jobs don't count as proper work experience.'

Perhaps you think...

Unless you spent your uni holidays doing something seriously impressive, employers aren't interested in any paid work you've done so far. Having casual work on your CV makes you look amateurish and unfocussed.

Reality check:

Most employers view any experience as good experience. However fancy or loser-ish your job title was, and whether the work was paid or unpaid, to employers it's all a 'plus'. Any experience demonstrates that you have a responsible attitude to work and that you have experienced life beyond academic institutions. In other words, it shows you can exist in and interact with the real world, not just in the uni bubble.

OK, so maybe your holiday job isn't quite as impressive as your friend's internship at a political think-tank in Washington DC or traineeship at a big City bank, but make no mistake – it still counts. Yes, even if you spent your summers au pairing, stacking supermarket shelves or litter-picking at Glastonbury, employers want to hear about it.

If you're worried your CV looks a bit thin, don't worry too much about it. You'll be surprised by how lenient most employers can be. For the most part, they're realistic. They know what graduates are like. They know that despite being nagged since school to use your holidays productively to beef up your CV, very few graduates actually manage it. They know that having fun just seemed more important. They know that getting proper experience meant thinking about your 'career' – and that you really didn't want to do that. They know that you stuck your head in the sand and dossed about doing as little work as possible. Or you took a job that paid all right, even if it didn't sound like a corker on paper – data entry, anyone? But that's OK. It's not amazing, but neither is it a disaster. Whatever work you've done, it's still something – and from an employer's point of view, it's definitely better than nothing.

So, just because your holiday job doesn't sound great to you, that doesn't mean you should downplay it to potential recruiters. And don't even think about leaving it off your CV altogether. Instead, careers advisers suggest you squint and look at it differently. There's a good chance you're undervaluing the experience you've gained. Even if your work experience doesn't seem related in any way to anything you might want to do in the future, it *has* taught you something.

The good news:

It means you do have something to put in the section on your CV marked 'Employment history'. And you're not as far behind other candidates as you think. In fact, if you invest a bit of time, you can even make your experience sound halfway impressive!

Crap job – brilliant experience!
Had the pleasure of doing any of these rubbish summer jobs? You'll be amazed at the skills you picked up…

Waiting tables/bar work
Public speaking, informing, explaining, persuading, advising, negotiation and conflict resolution, listening and questioning, concentration, cooperation, resilience, memory and recall, multi-tasking… Plus, having direct contact with customers shows you have been charged with the responsibility of presenting a positive image of the restaurant or bar.

Au pairing/babysitting
Informing, explaining, entertaining, empathy and sensitivity, persuading, social interaction, problem-solving, listening and questioning, organising, leadership, cooperation, planning, timekeeping… Also, being put in charge of children's well-being demonstrates that others have enormous confidence in your sense of responsibility. It says something that someone trusted you enough to leave their child with you.

Data entry/stuffing envelopes
Attention to detail, checking, timekeeping, consistency, accuracy, completion, psychological resilience, concentration, determination… Plus, demonstrating a commitment to a job that consists solely of tedious admin shows you're unlikely to dodge the small amount of admin that any future job might demand.

Reception work
Informing, explaining, social interaction, listening and questioning, sensitivity and empathy, cooperation, resilience, recall and memory, prioritising… Experience of reception work also shows that you have

Hey, we've all been there...

Casual jobs are a rite of passage. Just ask these stars:

* Whoopi Goldberg once worked at a mortuary, applying make-up to corpses.
* Bruce Willis was once a security guard at a nuclear power plant.
* Shania Twain, Sharon Stone, Pink, Amazon.com boss Jeff Bezos and actress Rachel McAdams have all worked at McDonald's.
* James Gandolfini – TV's Tony Soprano – once drove a delivery truck for soft drink company Gimme Seltzer.
* Brad Pitt was paid to stand outside fast food restaurant El Pollo Loco ('The Crazy Chicken') in a giant chicken suit.
* Former 007 Sean Connery has worked as an artist's model, a lifeguard and a coffin polisher.
* Charles Dickens worked in a factory, sticking labels on bottles of shoe polish.
* Demi Moore worked for a debt collection agency.
* Pierce Brosnan once busked as a fire-eater.
* Steve Martin worked in the Magic Shop at Disneyland, making balloon animals.
* *Nineteen Eighty-Four* author George Orwell washed dishes in the kitchens at a fashionable Paris hotel.
* Johnny Depp and Jack Black have both worked as telemarketers, selling products over the phone. Johnny flogged pens, Jack peddled audio tapes of whale sounds.

been entrusted as the first port of call for callers or visitors to the company, so you're likely to be highly presentable and professional.

Street fundraising for a charity

Informing, explaining, persuading, entertaining, challenging, social interaction, attention to detail and checking, public speaking… If you've had a job as a 'chugger', it's likely that you have first-rate 'people skills' and aren't shy.

Working at a festival/sports event

Teamwork, informing, explaining, persuading, social interaction, timekeeping, resilience, cooperation… This experience is particularly valid if you were interacting directly with the public (checking wristbands or selling ice cream) – since that shows you were trusted to be a 'face' representing the brand or event.

Myth: 'Hard to get into' means 'Don't bother'

Perhaps you think...

When considering your options, it's important to be realistic about which jobs are attainable and which jobs are so competitive that there's no point in trying. Choosing a job or industry that you're less excited about but is easier to get into will mean you're happier in the long-run.

Reality check:

Jobs or industries that are described as 'competitive' are tricky to get into, but not impossible to get into. Unfortunately, one doom-monger is often all it takes to put graduates off investigating a job further. But I have good news. If you ditched an idea that appealed to you just because one person, website, brochure or leaflet mentioned it was 'hard to get a foot in the door', un-ditch it. And, the next time someone suggests you find something easier instead, be prepared. Instead of taking their advice as gospel, ask yourself: 'Is this person an expert? Are they qualified to make this judgement?' Always make sure the person you're speaking to really knows their onions. Is this person actually involved in the job or industry you're interested in? Don't bin a good idea because of someone else's half-baked stereotypes.

Then ask yourself: does this person have a reason to persuade me against pursuing this job? Perhaps they want you to join their firm instead – or perhaps they just want to steer you towards their idea of what's best for you. Remember, many parents encourage their child towards the most stable professional life, simply because they want you to be spared any unnecessary upheaval and rejection.

For an accurate picture of a job that sparks your interest, you really need to speak to people who are currently employed in that line of work. Weirdly, you'll probably find they'll have much better news for you. Even in the most competitive industries, it's rare to hear someone say it's impossible to get in. Difficult, yes – but not impossible. They're far more likely to say that it takes a lot of hard work, or that you have to be really determined, or that you should grab every opportunity with both hands. It's up to you to decide whether you're prepared to put the work in.

If you are, then go for it! It's not my place to tell you you're not good enough to make it – I have no idea how good you are, or how determined you can be. Of course, there's always the chance that you might not quite make it. Or that you might take a job as a 'stepping stone' to that job and love it so much that you do that instead. Or you might reach your goal and realise it isn't what you want to do after all! But it's not the place of a doubting careers adviser, concerned friend or anxious relative to put you off pursuing your goal.

Until you're told several times by several people in that industry that you're not good enough to make it, I don't see anything wrong in trying. So, if you want to be a film producer, a sports journalist or an actor, this is the moment to go for it. If you aren't good enough, you won't make it.

If you are, you will. Sometimes, working out how to get into an industry is part of the test.

The good news:

If you've ever had an idea about a job you might like to do but had someone quash it immediately as 'too competitive', now is the time to go back to it. Besides, all the best jobs are 'hard to get into'. Would you really want a career in something that isn't competitive? If so, I hear they're always hiring traffic wardens…

> ## Myth: 'Today's graduate job market is tougher than ever before.'

Perhaps you think…

These days, everyone's been to uni. Because the number of people with some form of degree has rocketed in the last few years, and the number of graduate jobs hasn't, all graduates face a real uphill struggle to find work. That's why all the selection tests are so tough. Employers just have too many great candidates to choose from.

Reality check:

There are plenty of graduate jobs out there. If you're having a nightmare landing one, it's not because there aren't enough vacancies. Yes, the number of people with some form of degree has risen. And yes, the number of places on structured graduate schemes hasn't. But you're jumping to conclusions. Why? Because the supposed shortfall is almost certainly made up by an increase in other types of graduate jobs.

'In my opinion, the graduate job market is definitely not shrinking,' says Alistair Leathwood, managing director of recruitment consultancy FreshMinds Talent. 'When all grads hear about are job cuts and recruitment freezes, it's easy to forget to take into account the thousands of new jobs that have actually been *created* recently – and that includes graduate level roles.' Much of this growth has been in the technology sector, with the arrival of Google and eBay for example. In addition, think of all the new eco-companies; feel-good ethical retailers and green energy producers just didn't exist a few years ago. See? Brand new jobs.

If any scare-mongering stats float your way, treat them with caution, warns Alistair. And don't take news headlines at face value either. 'For a start, now that employers aren't allowed to specify the age of their desired candidate (or even, strictly speaking, whether they should have a degree) a 'graduate job' is impossible to define in absolute terms.' The point is how can anyone count these jobs when there isn't even a hard-and-fast rule for spotting them?

Even the 'facts' can't really be trusted, Alistair explains. 'The problem is that there is no one source of statistics about the job market. Everybody uses a different set of numbers – and figures can easily be selected to suit anybody's purpose.' What about the media scare stories about redundancies and recruitment freezes? 'Again, be suspicious. Just because a couple of departments in a couple of companies put their graduate recruitment programmes on pause, it doesn't mean there aren't still plenty of vacancies to be filled elsewhere. My advice is to forget about the stats and the headlines. I work with graduates and graduate employers day in, day out, and the truth is that good people get good jobs.'

Hey, wait a second, *you're* good! So where are all your job offers? If you're struggling to get that elusive 'When can you start?', Alistair suggests two possible reasons – and no, it's not because you're rubbish. 'First, graduates who consider themselves generalists or good 'all-rounders' tend to flock to the same jobs – the widely advertised, spectacularly paid, glamorous ones with household-name employers – so it's little wonder they're the group that says it's so hard to find a job. Second, employers are using more sophisticated selection techniques to spot candidates who don't really want, or understand, the role they're applying for.' In other words, if you're interviewing for jobs that don't really excite you and, ahem, didn't do quite as much homework as you should have done before that last interview, is it possible you're not as good an actor as you thought? If your heart isn't in it, recruiters can tell. And maybe that's the explanation for why you haven't had any joy with your job-hunt so far. Find a job you actually want, and you'll be far more convincing.

The good news:

The reason you aren't having any luck with your job-hunt has nothing to do with the economy, or the evils of our capitalist society. More than likely, it's because of something you are doing wrong. If that sounds harsh, it shouldn't, because in fact this is good news. It means the problem is easily fixable. You just need to change your approach. Alistair explains, 'Avoiding the scrum for the mainstream graduate schemes and applying for jobs you're actually interested in should dramatically increase your chances of landing a brilliant graduate job you'll love.' In other words, track down vacancies that are less widely advertised and watch your chances of success soar. And if it's a job you actually like the sound of, you'll be far more convincing in the interview. Now, doesn't that sound like a much better plan?

> ## Myth: 'I can't apply for a job unless I already know how to do it.'

Perhaps you think...

Employers expect graduate employees to 'hit the ground running'. Bosses don't have time to spoon-feed their staff. If you can't hack it, you'll be out on your ear.

Reality check:

No one expects you to be able to do a new job perfectly, from day one. How could you? You've been at university for at least three years. What most employers are after is potential – not knowledge. Don't believe us? The following list was adapted by The Careers Group from figures that appeared in *The Independent* and *The Guardian*. The Careers Group says these are the top ten qualities that recruiters look for in graduates, all of which are given equal weighting:

1. **Team working ability** – Can you work with other people?
2. **Leadership ability** – Can you handle being in the driving seat?
3. **Organisation, planning and prioritisation skills** – Do you think things through clearly before you get stuck into a task?
4. **Mental and physical resilience** – Are you strong enough to handle set-backs?
5. **Flexibility and adaptability** – Can you roll with the punches if circumstances change or things don't go to plan?
6. **Self-motivation, drive and commitment** – Do you 'make it happen' and press on, no matter what?
7. **Analytical ability** – Are you on the ball when examining detailed information?
8. **Decision-making ability** – Can you weigh up options and make sensible judgements?
9. **Communication and interpersonal skills** – Can you balance being honest with being tactful?
10. **Commercial awareness** – Do you have a basic understanding of how the industry works?

You'll see that nine of these are personal skills, only 'commercial awareness' is knowledge-based.

Yes, OK, in an interview, most employers do expect you to know a bit about the role, their company and their industry – but not because you'll need that knowledge to do the job. A basic understanding of what you're applying for shows that you understand what job you're potentially signing up for, decreasing the chances of you deciding you don't like it after all, and leaving after a week/month, so they have to recruit all over again, which is a giant hassle for them.

As for the job ads, they're usually more of a recruiters' wish list – the requirements are rarely set in stone (for more on this see 'The job spec – set in stone?' in Chapter 6). Even if the experience or abilities are presented as 'must-haves', they're often more like 'nice-to-haves'. If they like you and you're the right person for the job, they'll probably let a couple of things slide.

Employers aren't stupid: they know they'll need to train you up before you can do the job properly. What this involves will depend on a number of factors, including the size of the company and its training budget, the number of other new starters – mass training sessions work out as cheaper per head than individual training – and the nature of the job itself (how much is theory, and how much is practice).

What will the training be like? Again, it depends on the role and your employer. It could be a formal year-long course, or a small number of informal chats with various existing members of the company, or you might simply be given a reading list.

Whatever form it takes, this training will only be the start. In your first few months in a reputable company, you should be well looked after. That said, different companies will have different ideas about how structured your training should be. For example, smaller companies are likely to have a less formal approach than larger companies and expect you to use your initiative and pick things up as you go along, asking for help and guidance when you need it – and they're also more likely to be understanding if you make mistakes! Larger companies – where you may be one of several new starters – might provide more formal training before letting you loose on the job, in order to minimise errors once you start properly.

You should be given a clear outline of all the different aspects of your job, and shown how to do them. You'll most likely have a designated manager or mentor, who you'll be encouraged to approach with questions and concerns. They may also give you regular reviews to see how you're getting on.

The good news:

You can apply for jobs you don't know how to do but think you might be good at if the employer takes the time to teach you. Bearing this in mind should multiply the number of job options open to you.

> ## Myth: 'Eventually, your dream job will just "strike you"'

Perhaps you think...

If you don't yet know what you want to do long-term, it's a bad idea just to take any old job in the meantime. It's a waste of time getting experience in a field you might not even end up in. If you wait long enough the idea for your 'dream career' will just pop into your head.

Reality check:

Whatever the circumstances, waiting time is dead time. Every minute you spend lounging around on your parents' sofa, or killing time doing mind-numbing temp work, is a minute you're not spending trying out something new to see whether you like it.

If you've convinced yourself that lightning is about to strike any day now – forget it. I know that the idea that there's one perfect job for you out there is immensely seductive – rather like believing there's one perfect soulmate – but this sentimental belief can be hugely destructive. Sitting back and waiting for your dream job to come to you is just about the worst thing you can do and it's a dangerous game to play.

Why? Well, for starters, I just don't believe that this dream job exists. Even if you find a job you love for a while, you won't love it forever – you'll move on to bigger and better things. Or you might get your dream job and find you don't like it as much as you thought you would. Second, this dead time spent waiting for inspiration to strike can be seriously bad news for your CV – not to mention your bank balance. Third, this 'waiting for the big idea' mindset tends to prevent grads from looking for great first jobs (see Chapter 3), where you'd gain experience and perspective to help navigate your future later on. And finally, the idea of a dream job triggers unmanageable levels of panic, expectation and even paralysis in graduates like you. And I'd like you to be spared that torment, if possible!

When inspiration doesn't strike, all that will happen is you'll lose your confidence and motivation, and you'll still have no experience.

If you've been holding out for the big idea to strike, you need to shift your expectations and define a new goal. A much more sensible approach is to set out on the right path towards a fantastic first job – by which I mean your first proper job after uni. In this job, you'll be picking up new skills and bagging some great experience that will prove useful when applying for future jobs that you'll like even more.

The good news:

You're in the driving seat and you always were. You're not leaving your job-hunt up to the gods, or fate, or the stars. You are in charge of your destiny. You don't need a grand plan in order to 'make it'. Instead, have faith in your ability to make smart decisions as you go along. You'll end up where you want to be.

In Chapter 3...
Find hundreds of ideas for great first jobs you'll love.

Part 2:

The three-day plan

Inside: loads of jobs you'll love

NOTES

Chapter 3:
Day one

Lawyer, chef, musician? Whether you're stuck for ideas, swamped with them or contemplating a stab in the dark, you've come to the right place...

You will need:

- ☑ a pen
- ☑ a brain
- ☑ that's all.

The three-day-plan is an easy-peasy, step-by-step programme to help you assess what you're best at, what direction to go in and show you a clearer path ahead. A future that doesn't start with pages of job ads – a future that starts with you.

No more gazing at the online job boards, feeling uninspired and demotivated. No more having no idea where to start. And forget about feeling you should be shoehorning yourself into a job you know isn't for you.

You are *not* going to end up in a job you hate. Not if I've got anything to do with it.

In fact, I'm so confident in the genius of the three-day-plan that I am prepared to make you several guarantees. I promise that, just three days from today, you will:

- ☑ have pinpointed exactly what your unique, in-demand strengths are
- ☑ be brandishing a long list of possible jobs that you could do brilliantly
- ☑ be crystal clear on what your job priorities are (whether that's making a packet, working with people, making a difference...)
- ☑ have banished any pesky, half-baked stereotypes about possible jobs from your mind, so you're working from fact alone
- ☑ have a solid grasp of how most companies are structured, so you can see where you might fit in
- ☑ know exactly how to spot employers who will value your unique talents

☑ have matched yourself with jobs you'll love – not just jobs you can do

☑ walk away with one or two roles to start applying for immediately

☑ feel more positive and excited about your future than ever before.

So am I going to reveal your dream job?

Absolutely not. Why? Because, as you'll know if you've already read Chapter 2, I don't believe that such a thing exists. I think it's a load of old nonsense that sets ridiculous expectations and creates unmanageable levels of stress. Seriously, don't do it to yourself. That way madness lies.

Besides, I have a much better plan up my sleeve, a more sensible, manageable and realistic plan. I want to help you find the path towards a fantastic first job. By this I mean your first proper job after uni, where you'll be learning new things, bagging some great experience and generally feeling better about yourself in a matter of days. I know it doesn't sound as glamorous as your dream job, but trust me, searching for your dream job is like hunting for a unicorn.

What will your first job be? That really depends on you. But I think the best possible first job for you is one that is tailored to as many of your own unique talents as possible. You might not be in this job for longer than, say, twelve months, but to get the most from it, it should still play to your strengths. Not only will it make your first year out of university an easy, comfortable, enjoyable and encouraging experience for you, it'll also maximise the chances of developing your employability in ways you can use in your next role.

I believe in starting your job-hunt with you and your unique talent DNA. After all, *you* are the one constant in the series of jobs you will have during your lifetime. You are what all the jobs will have in common.

A good first job is simply a very good start.

The slacker's three-day plan

Really can't face thinking about your future? If all you want is a job, any job – and fast – here are five great starter jobs you could apply for today.

Just remember, this is probably only a temporary solution. Unless you harbour spectacular talent for the job and love it, a maximum of a year in one of these jobs should be long enough to get your head together before moving on.

Love chatting to people, doing deals and being on the phone?

Check out: media sales

'Some graduates with outgoing personalities can thrive in sales jobs but media sales is particularly popular, since it's perceived as touching on the TV, advertising and publishing industries,' says Susie Goldie, Head of the Careers Consultancy at C2, The Careers Group. While she wouldn't recommend it as a path into editorial work (side-stepping can prove tricky), a first job in media sales can be great experience for graduates with natural charm and a knack for clinching deals – and can really boost your confidence further. 'If you ever worked as a paid street fundraiser, then selling advertising space involves similar skills,' Susie explains. 'It will also give you the chance to develop transferable skills which could prove useful in your next job. In particular, your communication skills, especially on the phone, will be sharpened as you become practised at speaking to and negotiating with new contacts.' And there's more good news... 'Media sales salaries usually include a commission-based monthly bonus as an incentive for employees. So the better you are at the job, the more you'll earn.'

Enjoy meeting new people and sussing them out?

Check out: recruitment

'Working for a recruitment company can combine a range of skills,' explains David Winter, careers adviser at The Careers Group. 'You might have the opportunity to interview and assess candidates and develop your interpersonal skills as you liaise with clients. You'll receive expert training in 'soft sell' telesales too, learning the art of persuading companies to place vacancies with your firm. In addition, you'll get an overview of how some aspects of recruitment work, which might help you become more effective in understanding the job market, as well as honing your own CV and interview technique for when you decide it's time to move on. Recruitment can also be a good introduction to human resources work, training or career coaching.'

Get a kick out of troubleshooting, being super-busy, well-organised and knowing everything that's going on?

Check out: personal assistant work

'Some PAs – or EAs, executive assistants – are more like Deputy Managers,' says Laura Brammar, careers adviser at The Careers Group. 'They are involved in the day-to-day running of a department. PA work can be a great insight into the role of a manager and it gives you a fantastic overview of how an organisation operates. Usually, you'll be working with one senior executive and it's important to get on well with them. At times, you might almost need to be able to read their mind!'

Interested in what makes people tick?

Check out: market research

'A variety of big brands are commissioning increasingly sophisticated market research reports in a bid to understand more about their customers – and all sorts of companies put these reports together for them,' says David Winter. 'As a market researcher, you could be talking interviewees through a phone questionnaire, conducting a focus group – canvassing several people's opinions at the same time – or analysing the results back at the office. It can be a good introduction to the world of marketing and advertising. And some of the interviewing and analysing skills could be useful for future careers in social research.'

Get a buzz out of sharing ideas and travelling?
Check out: Teaching English as a Foreign Language (TEFL)

'This is a really popular choice for graduates who want an adventure whilst gaining some valuable experience for their CV too,' says Laura Brammar, careers adviser at The Careers Group. 'By the end of your teaching contract, you'll have experienced a different culture. Even better, you'll have picked up a range of fantastic transferable skills, preparing and delivering lessons to students of varying abilities, organising your marking schedule, and working with students and fellow teachers.' Grads who do TEFL stress that you get out what you put in. 'Most schools run a range of extra-curricular and social activities. The more involved you become with the students and other staff, the quicker you'll make friends and the more you'll take away from the experience when it's time to come home.'

Exercise one: Talent spotting

The reason

The first part of the three-day-plan is about pinpointing your own talents.

'But I'm talentless!' you cry, 'that's why I'm in this situation, I'm not brilliant at anything. If I was, I'd be doing it as a career. I can't play the piano like Jools Holland, or draw like Rolf Harris. I'm pretty bright, I suppose. And I'm OK at sport. But I'm hardly what you'd call talented.'

Nonsense, we're all good at something. You probably just haven't really thought about it before. Why would you? Until now, all your examiners, interviewers and tutors have focussed solely on what you've achieved and what you know. And, because you've been trying to impress them, you've told them all about what you've done and how clever you are.

But now, it's important that you start thinking about yourself as an individual. Because I think recognising what you're naturally good at is the first step to finding a future that's tailor-made for you. Forget squeezing yourself into a job that won't make you happy, or signing up with dozens of other grads to be part of this year's batch intake to a huge corporation in an industry you don't even understand. All this can be avoided if you take a bit of time now to discover where your true talents lie.

You can start by giving your personality room to breathe. You might have read articles about employers wanting 'blank canvas' graduates. I say there's no such thing. By the time you leave university, you have opinions. You have a personality and a sense of humour. So start thinking about what makes you a unique individual. You want employers who want you for who you are, not for who they think they can turn you into.

The experts agree. 'When you're taking your first real look at the job market, forget about what you know and what job you think you can get – and instead think about who you are,' says David Winter, careers adviser at The Careers Group. 'The smartest employers know they can always help you acquire more knowledge.' But they can't train someone to be charismatic when they aren't, or have brilliant ideas when they just don't. So, apart from academic abilities, what else do you bring to the party?

Ditch all that 'I'm a fast learner' stuff – that's not what makes you special. You have a personality – what are you like? Not just in the classroom, but outside it, too. What random things are you really, really good at – that other people suck at? Could you sell ice to the Eskimos? Are you doggedly determined? A brilliant listener? It's these qualities that should form the starting point for your job-hunt.

Why is it so important to put yourself first – and your employer second? Because playing to your natural strengths is the difference between being OK at your work and being outstanding at your work. If you're in a job that doesn't mesh with your personality, you will always struggle. Wrestling with a task you're naturally bad at will make you miserable. You'll be a square peg in a round hole. Choose a job that plays to your strengths and life will be far more fun.

Put simply, matching your work and your natural talents is the difference between being OK at your job and being brilliant at your job. It's the difference between doing your job and *loving* your job.

 ## The task

Instructions: circle the phrase or phrases that best complete the sentence:

Among my friends, I'm known for...

...having the gift of the gab.

...being a shoulder to cry on.

...thinking big.

...making life beautiful.

...my dogged determination.

...making things fun.

...haggling and bargain hunting.

...being uber-organised.

...knowing everybody.

...my sense of fair play.

...my no-nonsense approach.

...building and fixing things.

Read on to discover ways to work your talents...

 ## Warning:

The lists on the following pages are just intended to be a starting point to spark off ideas – they are not a comprehensive list of the *only* jobs you could do! I've only been able to list a teeny fraction of the zillions of jobs that are out there and have had to stick to broad umbrella job titles. And another thing: remember that many of these jobs can apply to lots of different sectors. Sales is a good example of this; after all, every company is selling something. Or project management: whatever industry floats your boat, employers will need people who are brilliant at planning, organising and running all sorts of projects. Even if none of these appeal right now, in days two and three you'll be doing your own research and will discover hundreds more related or 'spin-off' jobs that might just tickle your fancy.

If you circled... having the gift of the gab

Could you sell pizza to the Italians? Do people say you have natural charisma? Do you love the sound of your own voice? Are you funny, engaging, or just downright fun to hang out with? If you're a star when it comes to charming, persuading, coaxing and selling ideas to people, make the most of it. Few others share your flair for communication, especially with new people. It's a huge asset that's in hot demand in every sector.

Look for jobs that involve:

* presenting new ideas to people you might not know
* persuading people that your way is the best way
* translating complicated stuff into plain English
* using charm and wit to get what you want.

You might be brilliant at...

* Sales and marketing
* Advertising
* Public relations
* Fundraising
* Working in recruitment
* Teaching or training
* Politics
* Being a TV presenter or radio DJ

* Being a barrister
* Being a medical rep

If you circled… being a shoulder to cry on

Do people tell you you're a great listener? Are you someone that people come to for help when it all goes horribly wrong? Do you make people feel calm and safe? Do you give brilliant, insightful emotional advice – or genius, clear-headed practical suggestions? Not everybody has your talent for applying calm, systematic thinking to everyday problems – so if this is your thing, share it.

Look for jobs that involve…

* working with people on a one-to-one basis
* listening to individual cases
* giving advice or guidance
* or that require you to be 'the sensible one'

You might be brilliant at…

* being a counsellor or psychotherapist
* being a careers adviser
* teaching or training
* being a nurse or other health worker
* community or youth work
* being a social worker
* being a solicitor
* working for the Citizen's Advice Bureau
* working in human resources

If you circled… thinking big

Are you the person with the idea so crazy that it just might be brilliant? Do you enjoy taking risks – and basking in the glory when you pull off the impossible? Lots of companies want 'big picture' and 'what if...?' types like you. Whilst they know that not all your ideas will be practical, they're prepared to wait for the ones that are. Why? Because most people have strict boundaries around their thinking. Only a rare breed dares to dream.

Look for jobs that involve...

- ★ thinking up new ideas
- ★ predicting and planning for the future
- ★ working on large-scale projects
- ★ influencing policies that will have far-reaching consequences

You might be brilliant at...

- ★ being a strategist
- ★ being a lobbyist
- ★ working for a think tank
- ★ international relations
- ★ being a policy adviser
- ★ being an architect
- ★ being a property developer
- ★ being a TV producer
- ★ trend forecasting
- ★ product development
- ★ advertising
- ★ being a management consultant

 TOP TIP

Everybody loves a big thinker. Established companies will want you to help move their brand forward and small companies will want you to lend them your vision to help them expand.

If you circled... making life beautiful

Were you the person who turned their skanky first-year cell into a palace? Are you obsessed with how art, film, music and your surroundings make you feel? Are all your folders covered in doodles? Or, if you aren't good at creating art, perhaps you just *see* beauty all around you, where others walk on by? If this is you, then having an eye or ear for all things artistic puts you in a highly prized group.

Look for jobs that involve...

* using your artistic vision to create, design or collect new and beautiful work
* dedicating your time to bringing exciting new artists and their work to a wider audience

You might be brilliant at...

* being a photographer
* being an illustrator or graphic designer
* being a web designer or computer games designer
* being a fashion or interiors stylist
* being an actor or director
* being a song- or scriptwriter
* being a property developer
* being a landscape gardener
* being an arts director (editorial/advertising)
* being a talent scout for a record label
* working in wardrobe or costume design
* working for an auction house or art gallery

If you circled... my dogged determination

When the going gets tough, do you secretly relish the challenge? Are you a brilliant troubleshooter? If nothing gets you down, and your friends call you the Duracell bunny, most companies will want to hire you. Why? Because at work things can, and do, go wrong – all the time. So they're crying out for perky, can-do types like you. You might not think this is a particular talent, but it is. Everyone else might look like they're as determined as you, but they're running on empty. You, meanwhile, still have great wells of stamina in reserve…

Look for jobs that involve…

* troubleshooting and problem solving
* organising large long-term projects
* facing daily challenges
* future opportunities to lead a team

You might be brilliant at…

* being an NHS manager
* being an event organiser
* being a social worker
* being a charity fundraiser
* being a political party agent
* being an international development or aid worker
* being a management consultant
* working for a human rights organisation
* community or youth work
* being a trader
* working in regulatory affairs
* being an IT programmer or web developer
* being a project manager

If you circled… making things fun

Were you the class joker at school? When you give a presentation, do you open with a joke? Are you drawn to the lighter side of life? You'll be glad to hear that life after uni needn't be boring. All you need to do is find a job that allows you to use your light-hearted style to entertain and inspire others.

Look for jobs that involve...

* entertaining or inspiring reluctant people
* using charm and humour to get what you want
* presenting ideas to an audience
* future opportunities for managing a team.

You might be brilliant at...

* being a fitness class instructor or personal trainer
* being an actor or comic
* being a TV presenter or radio DJ
* being an events organiser
* working in tourism
* teaching or training
* community or youth work
* sales
* advertising
* being a computer games designer

If you circled... haggling and bargain-hunting

Will you spend ten minutes arguing with a Moroccan stallholder over the equivalent of 20 pence? Do you always get several quotes before getting your car fixed? Can you look around your bedroom and know you shopped around for the best deal on every item in it? Bargain-hunters are in big demand for roles that involve buying and selling. Everybody wants to get the most by spending the least – so if you can help them do that, you're a real asset.

Look for jobs that involve...

* ★ negotiating the best outcome
* ★ persuading and sourcing new business
* ★ doing deals
* ★ being in charge of budgets

You might be brilliant at...

* ★ being a buyer
* ★ working in corporate finance
* ★ being a management consultant
* ★ being a music, TV or film producer
* ★ being a fundraiser
* ★ being a sports or arts agent
* ★ being an events organiser
* ★ being a scientific research bid writer

If you circled... being uber-organised

Were you the only person in your year who handed in your dissertation early? Do you find it impossible to understand why some people are always ten minutes late? (Why don't they just leave ten minutes earlier?!) Do you like clear systems, rules and timelines? Then put your talents to good use – because most other people are a total shambles. If anything's going to get done, they need you around to crack the whip...

Look for jobs that involve...

* ★ planning and organising detailed information
* ★ clear-thinking and prioritising tasks
* ★ organising and delivering long-term projects on time
* ★ liaising with lots of different people

You might be brilliant at...

* being a personal assistant
* being an NHS manager
* being a project manager
* being a production manager
* being an editor
* being an MP's researcher
* being a charity fundraiser
* being an accountant
* teaching or training
* being a researcher
* working in audit and compliance

If you circled... knowing everybody

Did everyone at uni know your name, and did you know theirs? Were you always in on the latest gossip long before everyone else? Do you work the room at big parties? If you're the kind of person who understands that other people can be a resource, and you see your social network as an invaluable well of information, you'll be valued in a role that involves knowing how to coax facts or opinions out of people, and using them to your own advantage.

Look for jobs that involve...

* infiltrating social networks
* matching people together
* using (and widening) your own social network

You might be brilliant at...

* being a bar or club promoter
* being a celebrity agent
* being a journalist

* being a trend forecaster
* being an events organiser
* being a market researcher
* being a maître d'/restaurant/hotel manager
* working in recruitment
* working in public relations
* arts administration
* working in sales

If you circled... my sense of fair play

Do you always cheer for the underdog? Do you step in during a fight – or feel annoyed with yourself later if you don't? Do you hate it when those in power 'get away with it'? A keen sense of justice is one of the noblest motivators. If that's what drives you, do the rest of us a favour and make good use of your skills. You won't be short of people who appreciate your ambitions.

Look for jobs that involve...

* standing up for what's right
* protecting the disadvantaged
* bringing people to justice

You might be brilliant at...

* being a solicitor or barrister
* being an equality and diversity officer
* working for the police
* working for a consumer rights organisation
* working for the Citizens' Advice Bureau
* international development or aid work
* community or youth work
* working in risk management

* union work – working in industrial relations
* arbitration
* working in regulatory affairs

If you circled... my no-nonsense approach

Do you make decisions swiftly? Do you hate it when people make a fuss? Are you unafraid to speak your mind? If your practical, unsentimental style is the envy of over-emotional ditherers, expect to be welcomed with open arms in any role that requires straight-talking and cut-to-the-chase *sorting*.

Look for jobs that involve...

* practical decision making
* organising projects and events
* managing contracts and other staff
* keeping a level head

You might be brilliant at...

* being an office manager or personal assistant
* being a GP
* being an accountant or auditor
* being a nutritionist
* being an environmental health officer
* being a health and safety inspector
* working for the emergency services
* working for the police or the armed forces
* being a trader
* being a project manager

If you circled... building and fixing things

Do you always have a crack at fixing your leaking tap yourself, before you even think about calling in a professional? Do your friends ask you for help when their computer crashes? Do you know exactly how to get your friend's huge sofa up his tiny staircase? If you're hands-on when it comes to all things technical and practical, there are plenty of jobs that would play to your strengths.

Look for jobs that involve...

* investigating problems and sourcing solutions
* applying skills or expertise
* designing workable plans or products
* practical problem-solving

You might be brilliant at...

* being an aeronautical or automotive or mechanical engineer
* being a sound or lighting technician
* being a research or analytical scientist
* being an architect
* working in construction
* working in product development
* being a PA
* working in IT support
* being an IT programmer or web developer

2:00PM

Exercise two: Fun-finding

The reason

Whatever you end up doing, you're probably going to spend a serious amount of time working. Lots of people hate their jobs. If you don't want to become one of them, take the time now to ask yourself 'What do I get a kick out of?'

Of course, I'm not talking about the usual stuff, like hanging out with friends, going out on the lash, flirting with hot strangers... I mean those little golden moments when you do something your friends probably wouldn't enjoy – or wouldn't admit to enjoying – and you realise you're getting a bit of a buzz. As with your talents, you have your very own idea of what activities you find fun, exciting and rewarding. Whether you register them as a sense of achievement or just a cheap thrill, these can give you vital clues about the sort of work you might enjoy long-term...

 The task

Instructions: circle the phrase or phrases that best finish this sentence for you:

I'm the kind of person who loves...

...knowing exactly how much money I have in my account.

...throwing a party that's remembered for years to come.

...queue-jumping.

...helping friends resolve their differences.

...explaining things to others.

...getting others to play by the rules.

...harmless gossip.

...negotiating a discount.

...4 a.m. debates.

...spending hours in the library or lab.

...helping people in trouble.

...beating the clock.

If you circled... knowing exactly how much money I have in my account

So you're a practical realist who likes to know the facts? Plenty of jobs need people like you who are happy to plough through the small print if it means getting to the bottom of matters.

You might enjoy...

* being an accountant
* being a financial adviser
* being an actuary
* being a loss adjuster
* being a pharmacologist
* being an investment banker
* being a nutritionist
* being a solicitor
* working for the Inland Revenue
* quality assurance work
* being a researcher
* working in risk management
* working for a private security firm

If you circled... throwing a party that's remembered for years to come

Are you a social animal who's all about the glory? If you have a keen sense of fun, enjoy being where it's all happening and love the idea of leaving your mark, there are plenty of jobs that could fit the bill.

You might enjoy...

* being an events organiser
* being a wedding or party planner

* being a magazine writer or editor
* being a TV presenter or radio DJ
* being a bar or club promoter
* being a chef
* working in fashion
* public relations
* trend forecasting

If you circled... queue-jumping

OK, so it is a teensy bit unfair on your fellow queuers... But nice guys finish last, right? If you secretly like getting one over on other people, and aren't afraid to be a bit pushy if the occasion demands it, there are masses of jobs which you might get a buzz from.

You might enjoy...

* being a barrister
* being a trader
* being a lobbyist
* being a photojournalist
* being a tabloid journalist
* being a sports or celebrity agent
* politics
* sales
* being a medical representative

If you circled... helping friends resolve their differences

You can't bear it when your mates squabble – especially over something trivial. You can always see both sides of the argument so you're first in line to help them patch up their differences. If you're interested in 'aligning' people in tricky situations, and utilising your natural negotiation and peace-keeping skills leaves you feeling all warm inside, you can use this to your advantage in many different jobs.

You might enjoy...

* ★ being a counsellor or psychotherapist
* ★ being a mediator
* ★ being an account manager (PR/advertising)
* ★ being an occupational psychologist
* ★ working in human resources
* ★ working for the police or the armed forces
* ★ international relations
* ★ international development or aid work
* ★ trade union work
* ★ arbitration work
* ★ working in investor relations

If you circled... explaining things to others

Are you super-patient, with a knack for knowing how to express difficult concepts in a way that others will understand? If you enjoy using your talent for transforming information, there are many ways you can use it to make a living.

You might enjoy...

* ★ being a journalist
* ★ being a counsellor or psychotherapist
* ★ being an independent financial adviser
* ★ being a speech therapist
* ★ being a health visitor
* ★ being a social researcher
* ★ being a GP
* ★ teaching or training
* ★ being a public health information copywriter

If you circled... getting others to play by the rules

Do you enjoy upholding the law, and encouraging fair play? If you're a fan of systems and procedures, and are happy to be the rule-enforcer, lots of professions need you.

You might enjoy...

* being an equal opportunities or diversity officer
* being a barrister or solicitor
* being an environmental health officer
* being a health and safety inspector
* being a human rights campaigner
* being a surveyor
* working for the police or armed forces
* working in human resources
* working for a consumer rights organisation
* working for the Inland Revenue
* teaching or training
* working for an industry regulator
* working in compliance
* risk management

If you circled... harmless gossip

Fascinated by the way different characters and groups interact? If you love chewing the fat, and you're always the first person to know who's doing what, and with whom, make use of your natural urge to press your ear to the ground. Besides, it's not gossip, it's exchanging information!

You might enjoy...

* being a journalist
* public relations
* trend forecasting

* being a sports or arts agent
* being a social researcher
* being a PA/office manager
* being a financial analyst
* sales

If you circled... negotiating a discount

You have something they want – they have something you want. Do you get a kick out of striking a deal you're both happy with? Lots of people are terrified of head-to-head confrontation, so if you love it, make the most of it. Many jobs that involve negotiating and setting up deals are very lucrative, but there's also the chance to use your powers for good.

You might enjoy...

* being a fundraiser
* being an estate agent
* being a sports or arts agent
* being a buyer
* working for the police or armed forces
* international relations
* being a trader
* sales

If you circled... 4 a.m. debates

Are you sometimes so passionately committed to a late-night conversation that you fail to notice that the sun's coming up? People who love thrashing out ideas and opinions work best in professions where they're among other people like them. Or maybe you're just a night owl.

You might enjoy...

* being a lobbyist
* being a director (film/TV/theatre)

* being a columnist or critic
* being an academic
* being a gig promoter
* working for a think tank or research institute
* working in book publishing
* politics
* being an economist

If you circled… spending hours in the library or lab

Do you love losing yourself in tasks that require detailed information gathering? If you get a kick out of immersing yourself in research, you're likely to thrive in professions where you're given time and space to work alone.

You might enjoy…

* being a researcher
* being a financial analyst
* being a librarian or information manager
* being a solicitor
* being an actuary
* being an editor or proof-reader
* investment management
* translation work
* being an IT programmer
* being an analytical scientist

If you circled… helping people in trouble

Do you find it impossible to walk on by? Are you drawn to people or situations that need your help? If you're patient and caring, and get a kick out of improving life for the disadvantaged or standing up for the little guys, there are many sectors crying out for your help.

You might enjoy...

* being a charity fundraiser
* being a nurse or other healthcare professional
* being a speech and language therapist
* being an occupational therapist
* being an advice worker
* being a human rights campaigner
* being a health visitor
* working for a helpline
* working for the police or armed forces
* community or youth work
* working in human resources

If you circled... beating the clock

Did you hand in every uni assignment within an hour of the deadline? Were you a last-minute reviser for every exam you've ever taken – including finals? Eleventh-hour junkies need pressure to perform at their best, so seek out fast-paced working environments.

You might enjoy...

* being a chef
* being an investment banker
* being an events organiser
* working in live TV or radio
* news journalism
* politics
* investment management
* working for the police or armed forces
* working in management consultancy
* being a trader
* working in crisis management
* working for a private security firm

Fancy being your own boss?

A word about running your own business...

A lot of bright, ambitious graduates love the idea of working for themselves. And many of you will go on to do so – but probably not just yet, unless you have some seriously experienced advisers on board. The fact is that setting up your own company is a huge financial responsibility, which is why the smartest entrepreneurs start out working for others, watching their bosses intently and stashing away all that knowledge and experience for when they're ready to start up alone in a few years' time. If you follow their example and work hard, convincing financial backers you're a safe bet should be a doddle further down the line. In the meantime, of course, you'll hate being told what to do, but put up with it for as long as you can, safe in the knowledge that it's an investment for your future.

Exercise three: The single sentence approach

The reason

Even the most baffled graduates usually have a broad sense of what's important to them in a job and what isn't, says the team at The Careers Group, who meet thousands of you every year. After all, you don't need to know anything about the detail of what a job involves in order to know that you're only interested in jobs that are highly intellectually challenging, say, or that involve a lot of travel.

The single sentence approach can help some graduates – especially those who favour logic and reasoning and would describe themselves as a 'good all-rounder'. You may have found exercises one and two fairly challenging. Graduates whose decision making tends to be less structured might not find this next exercise so useful. This is because, unlike exercises one and two, the single sentence approach doesn't work with your personality.

There are, however, a couple of downsides I should mention first. One is that the many of the most common single sentence statements are extremely vague. For example, lots of graduates say, 'I want to work with people,' and mean completely different things. Where one grad might have social work in mind, another might be excited by forging professional and profitable business relationships. Both involve working with people – just in very different ways. For this reason, where a statement is too fuzzy to be helpful in your job-hunt, I've included prompt questions to help you focus more clearly on what you really mean by that statement, so you can take away something useful that's tailor-made for you.

I also should warn you that choosing your job based on one or two such arbitrary statements can seriously cut down your options, so don't be surprised if you don't like any of the jobs listed for you. If that's the case and you liked the sound of some of the jobs listed for you in exercises one and two, then stick with them. Console yourself with the fact that you've just discovered that your single sentence 'must-have,' the one thing that you considered crucial to you in choosing your job, isn't as important as you thought. You'd much rather have a job that suits your personality. For you, it's best to match your personality traits to work that suits you. You can always work out how to reach your life goals later.

 Warning:

Remember that your priorities are likely to keep changing over the next few years. What's really important to you now might not be in the future. In other words, these statements could quickly go out of date. So try and think about what might be important to you in the long-term, not just right now.

 # The task

Instructions: circle the two statements that best sum up what's most important to you in a job...

I want to work with people.

I want to make a difference.

I want to make lots of money.

I don't want to be stuck behind a desk all day.

I want to travel.

I want a job with variety.

I want to do something creative.

I want a job that's intellectually challenging.

Read on to follow your priorities to possible jobs…

If you circled... I want to work with people

You're in luck. It's quite hard to find jobs that don't involve working with people! But some jobs rely particularly heavily on people skills. To narrow your search down, it's helpful to think about what the purpose of this interaction is.

If you mean helping people with problems, you might enjoy...

* being a legal, financial or welfare adviser
* being a doctor, nurse or paramedic
* being a counsellor or psychotherapist
* being a speech and language therapist
* being a physiotherapist

If you mean developing people's potential, you might enjoy...

* teaching or training
* being a fitness class instructor or personal trainer
* being a careers adviser
* being a life coach
* community or youth work

If you mean developing professional relationships...

* being an account executive
* being a sales executive
* being a retail or media buyer
* being a management consultant
* working in business development

Other ways to scratch that itch:

There are too many to count! Almost all jobs involve working with people – so in reality the list of jobs is far longer than the one listed above. Unless you feel strongly that you would like to work with people in the specific ways listed above, it might be wiser to stick to the results of exercises one and two in order to generate ideas more tailor-made for you.

TOP TIP

Particularly like the idea of working in a small team? You might enjoy working for a small business, so don't limit your search to big companies. A first job at an SME (small to medium-sized enterprise) could be right up your street.

If you circled… I want to make a difference

Aw, aren't you nice? But what do you mean, exactly? Do you want to help people directly? Are you looking for an 'ethical' job? Or do you want to leave your mark in some way? Graduates who say they want to make a difference can mean all sorts of different things.

If you mean… helping people directly

Perhaps you find it rewarding to work with people one to one, or on the 'front line' (being the first point of contact for customers and clients)? Do you think you'd get a kick out of actually seeing the impact of your work on individual cases? Then look into…

* being a doctor or nurse
* being an advice worker
* being a counsellor or psychotherapist
* working for a helpline
* charity work
* clinical psychologist

If you mean... helping people indirectly

Do you think you could be more effective behind the scenes, improving the way things are done or campaigning for greater investment where cash is really needed? Then look into…

* politics
* being an NHS manager
* corporate social responsibility (public relations)
* being a charity fundraiser
* being a human rights campaigner
* being an ethical retail consultant

If you mean… helping animals or the environment

Perhaps your passion is for the natural world or ecological and environmental issues? If so, look into...

* being an environmental consultant
* being a vet or zoo keeper
* being an animal rights campaigner
* being a conservationist
* corporate social responsibility (public relations)

If you mean... leaving your mark

Perhaps you don't think you're cut out for helping others at all or maybe you'd just like your work to have some kind of permanent impact? If this is you, the world is your oyster. Do you mean you'd like to create something to leave behind – say, a film, book or even a building? Is it the idea of discovering something that does it for you? Would you like to be known for launching something new – a company or charity? Would you love to improve or shake up something that exists already? Or would you like to break a story that changes the course of history? If so, look into...

* being an artist, director or writer
* being a scientific researcher
* being an entrepreneur
* working for a think tank
* politics

Other ways to scratch that itch:

You might not mean making a difference in a societal sense. Do you mean that you'd be happy in any job where you can improve systems that aren't working, or share information with people who are going to put it to good use? If so, perhaps you could consider IT support, consultancy or being a press officer. Also, don't forget that wanting to make a difference needn't influence your choice of industry at all. For example, you could get this sense of 'making a difference' in other ways, perhaps by applying for more managerial roles later on in your working life, where you're coaching and developing junior members of staff.

If you circled... I want to make lots of money

Clearly, if you do anything well enough you can, in theory, earn a lot of money. Traditionally artists and writers don't earn much, but J. K. Rowling and Tracey Emin have done all right for themselves. That said, there are jobs where it's more common to bring home a serious pay packet. As a general rule, jobs that pay exceptionally well involve dealing in money or transactions. Most of these involve long hours without any whining. If you're up for that, go for it!

Look into...

* being an investment banker
* being a management consultant
* being an actuary
* being a company secretary
* being a stockbroker
* being a barrister
* being an IT consultant
* being a venture capitalist

Other ways to scratch that itch:

If you're prepared to wait a while for the cash to come in, you could consider less profitable careers – and just make sure you invest the money you make wisely. Or, you could spend the next few years gaining enough experience and knowledge (and making mistakes at other people's expense!) to set up your own business later on. Although it comes with its own risks, being an entrepreneur can be hugely profitable if you know what you're doing.

TOP TIP

Lots of careers don't start out paying well, but if you excel at what you do you could well be earning big bucks in a few years' time.

If you circled... I don't want to be stuck behind a desk all day

Scratch the surface and graduates mean all sorts of different things when they say this. Do you mean you literally don't want to work in an office environment? Or do you mean you don't want to spend all day every day in front of a computer? Would you be happy to do some computer work if it meant spending a lot of time working remotely, perhaps being on the road, or having frequent changes of scene?

Look into...

* being an airline pilot or flight attendant
* working for the police or armed forces
* working for the emergency services
* being an interpreter
* being a photojournalist
* being a bar, club or restaurant manager
* being an interior designer
* being a fashion stylist
* being a hair and make-up artist
* being an animal trainer
* being a field archaeologist
* being a gardener

Other ways to scratch that itch:

If it's just the idea of sitting at a computer all day that upsets you, don't discount all office work. Despite the IT revolution, some jobs still rely heavily on using the phone and meeting people in person. If person-to-person contact is your thing, look into recruitment, sales and journalism.

If you circled... I want to travel

In some jobs, travel is an obvious part of the role, for example, working as a holiday rep, pilot or travel writer. But remember, lots of other jobs can involve travel too. Check out jobs with 'portable' skills that you can use as a means to live and work abroad.

If you want a job based around travel, look into...

* being an airline pilot or flight attendant
* working for the armed forces
* working for the Diplomatic Service
* being a merchant navy officer
* being a travel journalist
* being a holiday rep
* international development or aid work

If you want a job that gives you 'portable' skills (and therefore freedom to travel), look into...

* being a chef
* being an interpreter
* being a sports coach or instructor
* being a TEFL teacher
* being a hotel manager
* being a holiday rep

Other ways to scratch that itch:

If you'd like to have the option to travel but don't want your whole job to be about travel, look for companies with offices all over the world.

Once you've got some experience under your belt in this country, your boss might want to send you to the Singapore/Sydney/New York office for a while...

If you circled... I want a job with variety

You fear routine and monotony – but what exactly do you want to be varied? Your daily to-do list, where you work or the people you work with?

If you mean a variety of task, look into...

* working for the police or armed forces
* journalism
* being a careers adviser
* being an event organiser
* being a project manager
* being a party or wedding planner
* being an arts administrator
* being a TV researcher

If you want a variety of place, look into...

* being a civil engineer
* being a quantity surveyor
* being a social worker
* being an estate agent
* being a management consultant
* being a medical sales executive
* being a photojournalist

If you mean a variety of people...

* being a retail manager
* journalism

* being a sales executive
* being a personal trainer
* teaching or training
* recruitment
* being a doctor or nurse
* being a management consultant

Other ways to scratch that itch:

Just because your first job isn't a smorgasbord of varied challenges with a constant flow of fresh faces, it doesn't mean you'll never have a job with variety. Once you've gained some expertise, it's likely you'll be assigned more interesting work and meeting lots of different people. When you're ready to go it alone, you might also consider becoming a freelance consultant. This means hiring yourself out to companies for one-off projects ranging from a month to a year or two. This kind of work is both lucrative and rich in variety.

If you circled... I want to do something creative

What do you mean by 'creative'? Being artistic or using your imagination and 'thinking outside the box'? Here are a few examples that meet each definition:

If you mean artistic, look into...

* being an illustrator or graphic designer
* being an art director (editorial/advertising)
* being a fashion photographer
* being a jewellery or fashion designer
* being an interiors designer
* being a writer
* being a film, theatre or TV director
* being a performer
* art or music therapy

* being an architect or property developer
* being a landscape gardener

If you mean using imaginative thinking, look into...

* teaching or training
* advertising
* journalism
* being a charity fundraiser
* being an events organiser
* being a government intelligence officer
* being a retail merchandiser
* trend forecasting
* working for a think tank
* being a barrister

Other ways to scratch that itch:

If you love being among creative people but know your own talents lie elsewhere, look at non-creative jobs working alongside creative people. For example, you might enjoy being a literary agent, working as a music PR, working at a gallery or being a PA to a celebrity.

If you circled... I want a job that's intellectually challenging

This is a slightly tricky one, as we all have a different idea of what constitutes 'intellectually challenging'. But there are many jobs that are traditionally regarded as requiring intellectual curiosity and good old-fashioned brain power.

Look into...

* being a university lecturer
* being an academic researcher

* being an investment analyst
* being a solicitor or barrister
* being a civil service administrator
* being a forensic scientist
* being an information scientist
* being a media analyst
* being a patent examiner
* being an engineer
* being an accountant

Other ways to scratch that itch:

If you want to use your brain but fancy getting out of the library or lab, you might want to consider 'brain-power' jobs in a more creative setting. For example, if you have a head for numbers, remember that banks and accountancy firms aren't the only people who need people like you. Who do you think is making sure art galleries don't go under? Or that films don't go over budget?

Need more ideas?

Remember, the lists I've provided in exercises one to three are very broad job types. There are zillions more specific role titles I just didn't have room for. For extra ideas about possible jobs, show your circled lists to the three most brilliant people you know. By this I mean people you know who have lived a bit, been around the block, have bulging address books and are always busy. People you respect or admire. This could be anyone: an uncle, a tutor, a friend of your cousin… Best not to pick your mum or dad though – their ideas will be loaded with bias and expectation. Show them which phrases you chose from the lists in exercises one to three and ask them what springs out at them. Do they have any other ideas?

What's your passion?

Got a burning passion for fashion, art, travel, the environment, human rights, music, film, TV, science, economics, food, sport or celebrity? It's worth thinking about how you could weave this into your work life. If your passion isn't something you feel you could ever make a living from, consider ways to marry your passion with your talent. For example, if you love fashion but know your talent is for detail and numbers, then why not look into working for a management consultancy which advises fashion retailers? Or you could even work directly for a fashion house. You might not have the flair to be a great designer, but you can make sure that the company's numbers add up and that its future is secure. If you love watching sport but can barely catch a Frisbee, why not put your organisational talents towards running sports events?

My three brilliant people suggested...

1. ....
   ....

2. ....
   ....

3. ....
   ....

I hope you've had a good day.

There's just one more thing I'd like you to do before you go and watch *Hollyoaks*.

 **Teatime task**

Look back on your results from exercise one and fill in the blanks:

My in-demand talents are:

1. ....

2. ....

3. ....

Which means I'll be good at these jobs:

1. ....

2. ....

3. ....

4. ....

5. ....

6. ....

Then look at exercise two and fill in the blanks:

I get a buzz from:

1. ....

2. ....

3. ....

Which means I might enjoy these jobs:

1. ....

2. ....

3. ....

4. ....

5. ....

6. ....

And finally, look at exercise three and fill in the blanks:

My priorities are:

1. ....

2. ....

Which means I could think about these jobs:

1. ....

2. ....

3. ....

4. ....

5. ....

6. ....

From the lists you've just written, pluck out the following:

Two jobs I'm definitely interested in:

1. ....

2. ....

Two jobs I quite like the sound of but would need to find out more about:

1. ....

2. ....

Two jobs I've never considered before but that might be worth investigating:

1. ....

2. ....

Two jobs I'd be good at but don't know exactly what they are:

1. ....

2. ....

Two jobs I'd be really good at but that I don't think are for me:

1. ....

2. ....

(TOTAL = 10)

Not feeling inspired? There's a whole world out there – are you seriously telling me there isn't a single job that you'd enjoy? If so, I'm not buying it. I have a sneaking suspicion that you're dismissing good options too quickly. But never fear, day two will soon sort you out...

In Chapter 4...
Make your own natural decision-making style work for you – not against you.

NOTES

Chapter 4:
Day two

Are you a 'squirrel', 'bull' or 'sheep'? Identifying your decision-making style will make your life a whole lot easier...

I was going to leave the section on decision making until day three – but I know what you're like. You probably already started filtering out ideas you didn't like the sound of after your very first glance at the exercises in day one. I know, because that's exactly what I would have done!

I blame the voices. The ones that start up in your head the minute you encounter a new idea. 'You'd rather kill yourself than do that job,' one says. 'What would your parents think if you did *that* for a living?' says another...

Most of these voices are downright unhelpful when you're still at the stage where you should be keeping an open mind, which is why you need to be ready for them. That's why I thought it seemed wise to look at this business of decision making *now*, before you start making bad decisions based on nagging doubts you should be ignoring.

The experts at The Careers Group say we each have our own style of decision making. I've done my homework, and identified three broad types of decision-maker. Whichever you are, it's too late to change. It's already in-built, hardwired, but don't worry. None is better or worse than any other, they're just different.

It would take hours of therapy to change your decision making type, and frankly, it's not worth it. Instead, I think it's a better idea to understand your decision making style, including the pitfalls associated with it, so that you can make the smartest decisions possible.

QUIZ – What sort of decision maker are you?

Circle the answer that's most like you:

You're in a restaurant and the waitress hands you a menu. Do you...

a. scan it, pick the dish that jumps out at you, often the 'Specials' – and close the menu in under a minute. Occasionally, you suffer from order envy, but usually it proves to be the right choice.

b. choose fairly swiftly and close the menu – until niggling doubts make you re-open it and go through everything you could have ordered, cross-referencing with what everyone else is having.
c. read it from cover to cover, rating each dish out of ten for tastiness, value for money and the probability they'll do something weird with one of the ingredients. You're less than half-way through when the waitress re-appears.

You're considering a trip to the cinema. Do you...

a. read a good review of a movie, and see that it's showing tonight at your local cinema. You might ask a friend, but if no one's available, you'll go alone.
b. have in your head a couple of films you'd like to see, but the friend you're going with thinks they sound rubbish so you go and see their choice instead.
c. buy a newspaper especially for the cinema guide and read all the reviews. You fancy one that's just out, but there's another film you missed that won't be on for long so you go and see that instead.

You book a holiday when...

a. you spot an ad for a great deal. You check your bank balance, find a friend who likes the sound of it – and book your flight and hotel within 24 hours. Carpe diem!
b. a bunch of mates have organised something and ask if you want to join the party. The dates aren't brilliant for you, but you'd hate to miss out on the fun.
c. you've asked everyone you know where (and when) they're thinking about going this year. You decide where to go by cross-referencing their plans with your availability.

Your idea of a good shopping trip is...

a. spotting something in the window, going in and buying it. Why shop around when what you want is right there?
b. taking a fashionable friend with you and asking for a second opinion on everything you like. That way, you can spend with confidence.
c. scouring the Internet in advance, and then trawling the high street. A systematic approach is the best way to be sure you've been thorough.

You picked your first choice uni by...

a. visiting a couple – and going with the one that felt most *you*.
b. waiting to see where most of your friends were going.
c. requesting as many prospectuses as you could, creating a spreadsheet of all your options, visiting as many universities as possible – and rating each across several key categories.

Did you answer...

Mostly a? You're a bull.
Mostly b? You're a sheep.
Mostly c? You're a squirrel.

If you're a bull...

You're a 'gut instinct' person, ruled by your heart, not your head. You know what you want when you see it and you rarely dither. You can't understand why some of your friends find decision making so hard. You just *know* what you want, and go for it. Pleasing others isn't particularly important to you. In fact, sometimes you suspect that you're considering a job *because* it would surprise your family and friends. When you're on good form, you're ambitious, and all about the glory. But when you lose your confidence, you come down hard.

So far, the three-day plan has been...

Too easy. Recognising yourself in the exercises was a piece of cake, but the job suggestions didn't give you many new ideas. You swiftly dismissed the jobs you know aren't for you, leaving a short list of jobs you'd previously considered. You're becoming impatient with this book already.

Bulls: what to do next...

You need to broaden your options and keep an open mind. Remember: considering a job you're not sure you like the sound of doesn't necessarily mean you'll end up doing it. I just want to make sure you give every possible option a fair hearing and because I'd hate to see you dismiss a strong contender without a really good reason.

- Look back at the lists you made for your teatime task at the end of day one. If you were feeling particularly dismissive when you made your list, you may not even have ten options.
- Re-visit the suggestions from the results of exercises one, two and three. Read them all again.
- This time, instead of dismissing the suggestions out of hand, cross reference them with the list 'Are you job stereotyping?' later in this chapter to give you an idea of the kind of rash judgements you shouldn't be making. For each job suggestion, ask yourself, 'If I'm saying No, *why* am I saying No? Do I really know what I'm talking about, or could some extra research be helpful?'
- If your gut instinct is based on half-baked ideas about what a job actually involves, ideas that come from a TV show, say, that's not a good enough reason to dismiss it as a job that fits with your talents, your idea of fun and your priorities. It's got to be worth considering – so put it back on the list.

- Read the section called 'The company x-ray'. It will show you that companies you may have discounted could in fact be right for you after all. This will broaden your options further.
- Make sure you have a full list of ten job options before you move on to the next section. Write your revised list of ten in the space provided at the end of this chapter.

Not sure if you're a bull after all? Then perhaps you're a sheep or a squirrel...

Words of warning

Susie Goldie at The Careers Group explains...

'Some people are brilliant at clear, quick decision making, and are often the envy of their indecisive friends. However, when it comes to thinking about possible jobs, over-doing their natural cut-to-the-chase attitude means they can dismiss possibilities without considering them properly. This means they narrow their options prematurely, and give themselves only a very short list of jobs to choose from. If this is your tendency, you should be particularly careful about stereotyping jobs without really understanding what they are. "Gut instinct" is all well and good – but make sure it is based on truth rather than rumour. That way, you can keep your options open and your outlook broader.'

If you're a sheep...

You're happiest making decisions when you have friends doing the same thing – or you know people who have taken that road in the past, like members of your family. Striking out alone isn't your idea of fun, and you can't understand why some of your friends take silly risks when there's a safer option available that guarantees a secure future. You also care enormously about what other people think of your choices, particularly your family and friends. Gaining and keeping their respect is crucial to you.

So far, the three-day-plan has been...

A bit tricky; spotting yourself in exercises one, two and three proved difficult. Exercise one felt especially alien, since you don't view yourself as 'talented'. You view yourself as more of a 'good all-rounder'. Some of the job suggestions were expected, but others were surprising, and made you think, 'Really? *Me*?' You're unlikely to pursue the more out-there suggestions – but still, it's nice to know you have options.

Sheep: what to do next...

OK sheep, what other people think is important to you, that much is apparent. It's fine to factor that into your decision making, but you also need to make sure you haven't dismissed anything that you would really like to investigate further.

- Look back to the lists you made for your teatime task at the end of day one. How many of those are influenced by what other people – your parents and your friends – would think of you for making those choices? How many of them are on the list just because that's what other people seem to be doing?
- Refer back to your results for exercises one, two and three. Are there any options that surprised you? That you quite liked the sound of, but dismissed on the grounds of what other people might think? If so, fish them out and add them back on your list.
- Read the section 'The company x-ray' later in this chapter. This will help you see that there are broader uses for your skills. For example, if you're considering IT jobs, remember that these don't only exist within IT firms, you'll find IT professionals working within every large company. So, if you're mad about music, you could look into applying to the IT department at a record label.

- Read the section called 'Are you job stereotyping?' later in this chapter and ask yourself, 'If I'm saying no to a job, am I sure I've got a good reason?' If you don't have a good reason, or feel you'd like to investigate the job further before you dismiss it, add that job to your list.
- Write your revised list of ten jobs in the space provided on at the end of this chapter.

Not sure if you're a sheep, after all? Then perhaps you're a bull or a squirrel.

Words of warning

David Winter at The Careers Group explains...

'Some people are real 'team players', they love being part of a group. The flip-side of this can often be their fear of isolation which makes them reluctant to take decisions which might be perceived negatively by others. They may make choices based on the decisions of significant other people in their lives. For example, they may take the same summer job as a friend, or follow a family profession. They can sometimes be drawn to popular or fashionable career options with large intakes, thinking that if other people are choosing this, it must be a good option. This doesn't necessarily mean that such a choice will be a bad one. However, some people who get swept along by the crowd into a particular career find themselves dissatisfied further down the line. They may eventually wish that they had thought more about what was right for *them*, individually.

If you're a squirrel...

You believe that the best decisions come from having all the facts. You invest heavily in investigating all your options thoroughly, so much so that some of your friends have suggested you go a teensy bit overboard. But you know that you could never make any decision, let alone an important one, based on half-baked ideas and poor research.

So far, the three-day-plan has been...

Slightly overwhelming. Finding yourself in exercises one, two and three wasn't too hard – it was the sheer number of job suggestions provided that left you feeling swamped. You now have so many choices you don't know where to start.

Squirrels: what to do next...

Squirrels benefit from learning how to narrow down their options – *sensibly*. You'd also do well to remember to give weight to factors that can't be rated out of ten, like whether you actually *want* to do that job or not...

- Revisit your lists from the teatime task at the end of day one. Did you want to cram in more jobs than I gave you space for? Don't worry, I'll help you narrow it down.
- Go back to the results of exercises one, two and three, and carefully read the paragraphs describing what you're like. Really think about your skills and what you value in yourself and in a job, before you even look at the possible jobs listed.
- Cross reference your results from the three exercises. Keep a tally of how often each job is mentioned.
- Have a look at sections 'Are you job stereotyping?' and 'The company x-ray' to make sure you're making decisions based on fact rather than fiction.
- Write your revised list of ten jobs in the space provided at the end of this chapter. The jobs that keep coming up should be at the top of your list, in positions one to seven. If there are any random ones that have only come up a couple of times but that you really like the sound of, write them in spaces eight, nine and ten. (Yes, simply liking the sound of them *is* a good enough reason to put them on the list!)

- Struggling to limit it to ten? Don't cram in more. Remember, you can always come back to your lists later – once you've done some more research – and replace ones you've decided against with others that you prefer the sound of.

Not sure if you're a squirrel, after all? Then perhaps you're a bull or a sheep.

Words of warning

Laura Brammar at The Careers Group explains...

'Some people need to gather and analyse vast amounts of information in order to help them make their decisions. Performing thorough research before reaching a conclusion is almost always a good idea, and few people do enough. However, sometimes people can become obsessed about knowing everything. Sometimes, more and more facts will not make a decision any clearer, especially if you are not able to evaluate the relative importance of different pieces of information. This hunger for data may be because they doubt their own judgement or because they like to be 100 per cent certain or they just feel that there is something else out there which has so far eluded them. When dealing with careers it is impossible to overcome every uncertainty, cover every possibility and iron out every risk. Often life is about taking a calculated gamble and being prepared to deal with whatever consequences result.'

11:30ᴀᴍ

Are you job stereotyping?

On day one, you looked through lists of possible jobs for you to investigate, tailor-made to your own natural fabulousness. Some of them might have caught your eye, but I suspect there were others that you dismissed instantly. But what was your thumbs-down based on?

Rejecting a job once you've researched it properly and feel it isn't for you is absolutely fine. I'm all for refining your list, as long as you really understand the job that you're dismissing.

On the other hand, if there's even a slight chance you're basing your impressions of it on something as silly as something someone once told you at a party, or the fact that the one person you know who has a job similar to that is someone you can't stand, I think it's worth investigating it further. If you still don't like the sound of it, then by all means bin it.

Of course, we're all guilty of making decisions about jobs based on half-baked ideas about what they actually involve. We make sweeping statements about that type of work, using stereotypes and prejudices that spring from twisted, biased or fictionalised 'evidence'. It's an easy thing to do. But it's also a dangerous thing to do.

Think about it: wouldn't it be awful if you accidentally swept aside a job you would have loved?

The aim for the rest of day two is to make sure you haven't chucked out a job for being *boring*, for geeks or too much pressure when, with better intelligence to go on, it could have been a role that suited you down to the ground.

The 20 most common job stereotypes

Not so fast! Don't bin a great job because you don't know what it is. Get your facts straight first...

1. 'Journalists are insensitive and pushy door-steppers'
They get a bad rap, but news and celebrity reporters aren't all bad – is war correspondent Rageh Omar a low-life? I think not. Besides, front-line reporters are only the tip of the iceberg. Journalists can specialise in travel, health, fashion and beauty – and don't forget the editors back at the office, who commission and refine the work reporters send in.

2. 'A career in IT means working in a basement'

OK, most IT departments don't have the most glamorous offices, but you needn't be stuck in them. Companies designing and testing computer games can be great fun to work for, or if you get a kick out of technical troubleshooting, you could work for an IT support firm that helps lots of smaller companies, which might mean popping in to their offices to sort things out when they go wrong. Many jobs in IT involve staying up to date on the latest technology. If you're always eyeing up the latest gizmo on the market, and are fascinated by the high-speed growth and potential of the Internet, IT could be for you.

3. 'Advertising is all about selling people products they don't want'

Yes, the aim of advertising is to shift more stuff. But the best in the business frequently go beyond that, by changing the way people think about something. A fantastic ad can be remembered for years. And there are other things you can advertise, other than 'stuff'. Charities, films and exhibitions need promoting, too.

4. 'PR is all about long lunches and calling people "darling"'

People who work in public relations try to control the kind of news stories that are written about a company, product or person. The best approach depends on the nature of the client. It's a big challenge, and it's hard work. It can also be very fast-paced: crisis management PR can be extremely exciting. And it isn't just fluff, you can do PR for a charity, and serious heavy-hitters like the government use PR services. Now that big companies are realising that 'green' business means good business, a growing branch of PR is within corporate social responsibility (CSR).

5. 'Being an entrepreneur means being a wheeler-dealer'

Running your own business doesn't mean working out of a yellow three-wheeled van, ducking and diving. And, with lower running costs than big firms, small businesses can make you serious money, as long as you have a solid idea and know what you're doing. The best entrepreneurs don't go straight into it though. Instead, they take first jobs in small companies or departments, soaking up knowledge like a sponge and making their mistakes on someone else's time whilst still being paid. When they have an idea for a business, they take their experience and their savings, and start up alone.

6. 'Sales means flogging double-glazing'

Sales is one of the broadest job categories there is – and no, it's not just about knocking on doors and cold-calling irate customers. Every business needs a sales team – they're the people who go out and tell people about the product or service the company is offering. Without them, the company won't bring in any money. The best sales people are confident without being aggressive, and use personality, judgement and humour to charm potential customers. They are also the ones in charge of negotiating a deal everyone is happy with.

7. 'Working in the City means "selling your soul"'

Yes, a City job means working hard in a world that's all about making money for other people – and yourself. But they trade in stocks and shares, not souls. If you love the buzz of doing deals and making a profit, the money markets could be the perfect place for you.

8. 'Working in television means "dumbing down"'

OK, reality TV has given telly a bad name in recent years. But things are about to change again, as the networks face a new challenge – one that needs brains like yours to solve. The popular, lowbrow shows make money, but decrease the channel's reputation and power. What's the answer?

9. 'Law is all about getting crooks off the hook'

Defending serious charges is just one very specific area of criminal law. There's also family law, employment law, human rights law, intellectual property (i.e. copyright) law, corporate law and media law. If you love an intellectual challenge and getting stuck into detailed research, it's worth investigating further.

10. 'Working in fashion is frivolous'

While it's true that glamorous people work in fashion, that doesn't mean that the job itself is frivolous, and if it is sometimes, it isn't all the time. Fashion editors and stylists do spend their time sifting through clothes and choosing their favourite picks – but it can be hard work too. Fashion assistants spend a lot of their time on more mundane tasks, such as asking stores and designers to lend clothes for shoots, and then sending them back once they've been photographed. Fashion shoots often involve taking long flights for very short trips and working long, knackering days when you get there.

11. 'Politics is for people without morals'

The media give politicians a hard time – and with good reason. But that doesn't mean everyone involved in Parliament is crooked. It sounds cheesy, but most people get into politics because they think the country can be run better than it is at the moment. Remember, there are hundreds of exciting behind-the-scenes jobs in politics. You don't have to be an MP – look into lobbying, think tanks and research roles.

12. 'Teaching means dealing with annoying kids all day'

Some children can be challenging, but working with them can be inspirational and rewarding too. It also depends on the subject you teach – creative and physical subjects can be more fun and varied, with the chance to get involved in projects outside the classroom. If you really can't handle little ones, have you considered teaching or training adults? Remember, your subject matter needn't be traditional academia. If you work in human resources or for a separate corporate training company, you might be teaching adults on subjects like conflict resolution or teamwork skills.

13. 'A PA is a glorified secretary'

Personal or executive assistants are vital to the senior people within a company. They manage their boss's diary and field his or her calls – but that's not all. Most PAs are regularly entrusted with sensitive and important information so it can be a great way to gain first-hand experience of how companies are run at the very highest level. A good PA knows everything and can anticipate anything. Far from being 'just a secretary', many graduates are surprised to find that PA work can be a great first job. Oh, and the pay isn't half bad.

14. 'Accountancy is just number-crunching'

Yes, being an accountant means having a head for detailed figures. But it can also involve advising clients on economic risk and how changes in the law might affect them financially. And you needn't work for huge corporations, small businesses need accountants too.

15. 'Working for the NHS is a nightmare'

The health system is rarely out of the news and is likely to remain under scrutiny – but improvements are being made. Big changes are happening in the NHS and dedicated non-medical health professionals, such as health service managers, are busy transforming government policy into practical, visible improvements for patients. Working in healthcare can also be extremely personally rewarding: saving people's lives, supporting patients through recovery and delivering babies.

16. 'Human resources is just about pen-pushing'

If HR professionals seem to rely heavily on systems and procedures, it's only for our own protection. It's important these safety nets are there for when things go wrong between employee and employer. But systems are not the sum total of HR's work. The more interesting stuff, like 'conflict resolution', is done discreetly so you never get to hear about it. In addition, it is possible to specialise in any of a wide variety of areas, including training and development.

17. 'A job in construction means wearing a hard hat'

In fact, construction is one of the fastest growing industries in the UK, covering an increasingly diverse range of projects. Working in this world could mean being a surveyor, assessing the environmental impact of new developments, promoting eco-housing, planning massive regeneration projects or even fixing installations at the Tate Modern.

18. 'Working for the police and armed forces means dodging bullets'

Not necessarily, there is an enormous network of support staff behind the front-line work that police officers and the armed forces carry out. For example, did you know that the army employs huge teams of lawyers, engineers and IT specialists? Or that the RAF recruits air traffic controllers – not just pilots? While most jobs within the police and armed forces require successful applicants to complete basic police or army training, in some cases this can be as little as four weeks.

19. 'Being a scientist means wearing a white coat'

Science careers are incredibly varied; you could be conducting obscure investigations of specialised areas in academic isolation, or working as part of a dynamic team under commercial pressures to develop products that will have an impact on the everyday world. Aside from research or analysis, there is also product development, quality assurance, patent work, technical writing, scientific consultancy or scientific policy.

20. 'The Civil Service is boring'

The range of roles within the Civil Service is vast. It doesn't just mean sitting at a desk in Whitehall. As a civil servant, you could work for the Cabinet Office, the Crown Prosecution Service or even the Government Communications Headquarters (GCHQ), which is responsible for detecting and preventing international terrorism. Still think it sounds dull?

Debunking the job jargon

Graduate job seekers hear these five terms a lot – but do you really know what they mean? What exactly is...

...management consultancy?

This is a service offered to organisations who want to know how to run elements of their business more effectively. Often, a management consultant (or a team of management consultants) will be sent out to work 'on-site' at the client's offices. Once the existing systems, processes and figures have been assessed, the management consultant reports their findings back to their client and advises on how things could work better. If the client agrees to take their advice, the consultancy might be assigned to help them make those changes. Because private companies are prepared to pay a lot for this kind of expertise, management consultancy for big businesses tends to be particularly well paid.

...investment banking?

This is quite different from management consultancy, even though graduates often lump the two together under the uber-vague term 'working in the City'. It's complicated stuff but, in basic terms, investment banks advise their clients, usually other big companies, on how to make money. Specifically, they might brainstorm ways that a client can grow or tap into new customers, say, in other countries, or advise them to merge with other companies for strategic reasons – 'mergers and acquisitions'. Carrying out these changes involves lots of different people. Some have the ideas, some negotiate the deal and others find the client the money to make it happen, usually by arranging a loan. Whatever part they play, all investment bankers need a solid understanding of economic and industry trends and developments within the financial markets.

...a researcher?

Being a researcher means something different depending on which industry you're in, although usually it involves carrying out some sort of detailed, front-line investigation. In pharmaceutical companies a researcher might run tests for new products. In a TV company, a researcher might find people to come on to chat shows and tell their stories. In banking, it can mean looking into companies and analysing their performance and risks. In recruitment it can mean something different altogether; a researcher at an executive search firm (or head-hunter) is paid to map a given job market, pinpointing that industry's rising stars.

...media sales?

This involves selling advertising space, anywhere you see or hear commercials. For every ad you encounter, a deal has been struck behind the scenes between the person selling the advertising space (on behalf of the magazine, TV channel or radio station) and the person buying the space (on behalf of the advertiser). Much of the work is done on the phone, but media sales isn't about 'cold-calling' people who aren't interested. Media sales teams build long-term relationships with their main advertisers and their work involves not only presenting a possible deal, but also a large element of persuasion and negotiation so that both parties are happy with the end result.

...a buyer?

A buyer doesn't just shop for a living – well, not exactly. In retail, a buyer is responsible for selecting the range of products or services that a store will offer in the coming season, whether we're talking about food, fashion, computers, homeware, mobile phones or financial services – anything you see being sold to consumers. Being a buyer isn't just about being given a budget, choosing nice stuff and maintaining relationships with suppliers – you also need a head for numbers (sales figures) and a nose for what will sell (which means staying on top of changing consumer trends). A good buyer will also be an expert negotiator, to secure the best possible deals for their company. As well as retail buyers, there are other types of buyers, including industrial or construction buyers (who buy equipment for large companies) and media buyers (who buy advertising space).

TOP TIP

Always find out exactly what the job is before you go for an interview – d'oh!

The company x-ray

Even if you have a bit of experience under your belt, it's unlikely you have a full view of the way that the different departments of a company fit together. Record labels don't just hire musicians. Property firms don't only recruit estate agents. And Oxfam don't just employ people to dig wells.

Every company is different – but most of them share these basic components. The name given to each may differ from one company to another, and smaller companies may combine some roles into one. From Microsoft to British Airways and SonyBMG to Innocent, if you cracked open any company, you would expect to find many of these elements inside.

The 'footsoldiers'

These are the people who actually deliver the service that the organisation offers to its customers or clients. In other words, they actually *do* what the company does. At a fashion house these are the people who design and create the clothing. At an architecture firm it's those who draw up the building plans. At a newspaper, it's the people who write, edit or design the pages.

Sales

This is the team of people who sell what the company has produced or bought to the customer or client, either directly or through an intermediary.

For example, at a manufacturing company, these are the people who agree a price to sell large numbers of their product to a retail chain, who will then sell them to the customer.

Administration

From filing and data entry to personal or executive assistants – the people who handle the nuts and bolts paperwork, databases and administrative duties that must run smoothly for a company to function effectively.

Accounts

Accounts are the money-men and women who know exactly how much is being made – and spent – at a company. They process invoices, pay bills, calculate tax returns, pay employees, plan budgets and make financial forecasts about how the company might expect to grow (or not) in the future. Larger companies might have a separate payroll department dedicated to paying the company's own staff.

IT

As well as handling all helpdesk enquiries the IT department maintains the company servers, installs upgrades and makes changes to the systems. For example, if a new office is being opened in another part of the world, the IT department will make sure that all the staff can share resources.

Operations

These are the people who look after the 'nuts and bolts' of the organisation – usually, they're responsible for the effective production and delivery of a company's goods or services to their customers, day to day. Clearly, the nature of this job depends on the organisation it's within. For example, a job in operations for a retailer might include planning and implementing delivery schedules so that the new lines are in stores at the right times, while working in operations for London Transport could mean ensuring that the tubes and buses run on time and are properly staffed.

Strategy

The people paid to worry about the company's future – and plan genius new ways to make sure it continues to grow and make money.

Marketing, Public Relations and Advertising

The marketing and PR teams are in charge of promoting the company and its products or services through the media, so that customers have a positive impression of them. A company's advertising staff will not make their ads themselves – they hire specialist agencies are that for them. But they do oversee this work and make sure the finished advertisements are seen in the right places (the best TV channels, magazines, etc) for the best price.

Human Resources

The people who organise training, recruitment, redundancies, employee performance reviews and holiday and sick leave. They also handle employer/employee disputes if things turn sour.

Legal

A team of specialist lawyers who know the company inside out and make sure it is not exposed to any – potentially expensive – loophole risks. Sometimes they will be permanent employees of the company – other times a separate legal firm will be paid to look after the company's legal affairs. Depending on the nature of the company's work, the legal department might draw up contracts between the company and its clients, again to reduce potential risks.

The Board

A mixture of the company's most senior figures and hand-picked experienced external advisers, this group meets several times during the year to discuss and vote on the biggest decisions the company needs to make.

 Teatime task

Having re-assessed your lists – and, bearing in mind the tailor-made advice for bulls, sheep and squirrels – fill in the following blanks:

My favourite 10 jobs (in no particular order):

1. ....

2. ....

3. ....

4. ....

5. ....

6. ....

7. ....

8. ....

9. ....

10. ....

In Chapter 5...
How to suss out your options without getting swamped.

Chapter 5:
Day three

Now you have a good few options, it's time to take a closer look at what each actually means...

You'll remember that your teatime task at the end of day two was to produce a list of ten possible job ideas that might suit you. For some of them you might need further training but they are basic ideas for giving you a bit of direction towards a brilliant first job that would be a sensible and valuable next step for you.

Remember, you won't necessarily stay in that job, or even that industry, for the rest of your life. In fact, you might only be there for a year or so. But that would be OK, because you'll still have learnt more than you would have done staying in temp work or at your old holiday job. You know that you can always change jobs and it's not the end of the world.

Looking at your list of ten jobs, you might well have a couple of favourites, and a couple that you're going off a bit already, even since yesterday. The aim for day three is to reduce this list of ten down to just one job for you to start applying for and two reserves, if you really can't decide.

I don't want you to sit staring at your list, trying to work out which is your 'dream' job. Remember, there's no such thing. On your list, there are probably several jobs you could choose to pursue, and be equally happy in for a while. There are no right or wrong answers – I just want you to choose the one you feel most positive about. If it doesn't work out, you'll do something else.

You could, of course, pursue several jobs, and see which one you get and just let fate decide, but I wouldn't advise it. Look closer and you'll see there are several reasons why the 'scattergun' approach isn't as smart as it seems...

1. Greater focus means more free time. Once you start the process of applying for jobs, you'll realise how time-consuming it is. Researching one industry for several interviews is a smarter use of time than researching three industries for three

interviews. It's so much work that you're likely to get de-motivated before you've made any real headway.

2. By focussing your job search on just one role, you'll learn more about it with every application you fill in and every interview you attend. You'll find your knowledge grows cumulatively. You'll find you can use information you've picked up from one interview to help you answer questions in another with a different employer. This won't happen if you search for several different roles all at once, plus, you'll get really confused.

3. Recruiters can tell if you aren't really committed to doing the job you're applying for. Remember, their questions are designed to weed out people who might not stay in the job for long, so you're going to have to be very convincing to win them round.

4. You can always change your mind if you go to a few interviews and decide your 'first choice' job isn't for you after all. Your second and third choices will be there for you to fall back on.

 The tasks

Task 1

Since you're only going to apply for one type of job, and you have ten at the moment, you've clearly got some work to do, deciding which to plump for. Before you go any further, I suggest you shrink your list of ten down to a mere five. Be careful not to stereotype jobs, and make sure you keep jobs that you like the sound of, but need more information about in order to be sure. Now half its original size, your list will instantly feel more manageable for the next part of your challenge.

Task 2

Now you need to trim your list of five – this time, down to just one job type (oh OK squirrels, with two reserves, if you really need to). To make an informed choice about which this should be, you're going to need more information.

And to find that information, you're going to have to do some research.

Don't groan and give up – you're so close to the finish line now! Trust me, if you press on, you'll be glad you did. Besides, I haven't hung you out to dry entirely. In anticipation of some heel-dragging at this stage I've put together a survival guide for each of you, with advice tailor-made for bulls, sheep and squirrels. Armed with this, you should find both tasks far simpler than you expect.

And my generosity and thoughtfulness doesn't end there. For further help with task two, I've provided structured questionnaires to keep you focussed when you come to the research bit (which can be overwhelming if you don't show it who's boss). Now that I've gone to so much trouble to help you, I will consider it a personal insult if you don't at least give it a go.

And remember, it is *your* life we're trying to improve here!

Advice for bulls

The good news...

You've already done the scariest part: generating ideas that you liked the sound of. The next bit, deciding *between* options, isn't something you feel frightened of or stressed about. Plus, unlike the other types, you take risk and uncertainty in your stride so won't be put off a good option because it's competitive or a long shot.

The not-so-good news...

Your tendency towards daring, intuitive decision making means that of all three types, you're the most likely to make a snap decision and ignore other strong options or opportunities. Plus – as you discovered in day two – you're also vulnerable to being misled by emotional reactions to cues that are not really significant, such as liking or disliking a single representative of a particular profession. In other words, stereotyping based on dodgy information. You're also likely to become bored half-way through your research so will need to crack on if you're going to get through all five.

Expect to find Task 1...

Relatively easy – your 'gut instinct' will guide you quickly towards your firm favourites.

Make Task 2 work for you by...

Seeking out people to talk to about each career, who will give you real, honest advice – do you already know someone who works in that world? Or perhaps you know someone-who-knows-someone who does? Thinking positive is great, but it's important you work from fact, not hearsay. Those rose-tinted glasses have got to go.

Don't forget...

In task 2, to give each of the five a chance to impress you, before you dismiss them. If you get your heart set on a particularly competitive field, remember that there's a difference between accepting risk and ignoring risk. While a positive, 'can-do' attitude is great, an arrogant attitude ('How hard can it be?!') can be unrealistic and short-sighted.

If you're really struggling...

Already going cold on all ten jobs? Return to day one and generate new ideas or spin-offs from your existing ten. (Remember, there are zillions of jobs out there – I've only listed the broad titles.) Also ask your three brilliant people to help.

Advice for sheep

The good news...

The idea that it's a bad plan to choose careers based on the views or wishes of other people isn't necessarily true for everyone. For some people the rewards of cultural or family acceptance, or years of reliable, well-paid employment are more important than individual job satisfaction. You're also naturally risk-averse, so are unlikely to choose a pie in the sky option, or make rash decisions.

The not-so-good news...

The danger in being too accommodating to others' views is that you could end up making decisions that will make other people happy but will leave you feeling dissatisfied and unfulfilled. The danger in being too cautious is that you try to avoid any risk whatsoever. You can't avoid risk entirely in job decisions. The world of work is a shifting and unpredictable place. By trying to find the most secure options you may make too many compromises and end up doing something you don't enjoy.

Expect to find Task 1...

Perhaps slightly squirm-inducing – especially if it means losing options that you know would make others happy (or keeping those that would make others *un*happy). Try and keep a mixture of options that would please others and options that you find appealing personally – at least until you know more about what each one really involves.

Make Task 2 work for you by...

Keeping the list of your 'rejected' five jobs to hand, once you start researching your chosen five, check back and ask yourself whether there are any on the rejected list you wished you'd chosen to research further. Did you have a 'secret favourite' that didn't make the cut? If so, resurrect it.

Don't forget...

Before you start Task 1, make sure you sit down and speak to the people whose opinions matter so much to you. Explore their true expectations. If your heart is set on a job that you fear they won't approve of, you might be surprised to discover that they can be persuaded to see things from your perspective after all, especially if your decision has been carefully thought out and you can show it is not just an act of rebellion. And remember, your decision might impact others, but the person it will most affect is you.

If you're really struggling...

Put pen to paper – it can be helpful to see all the push/pull factors in black and white. Think about the consequences of choosing each option and identify the important people in your life who may be affected by your choice. Make two lists:

List 1: Impact on you (external) and impact on others (external).
What are the observable consequences – to you and others – of choosing this option? Consider lifestyle, working hours, travel, relocation, etc. Who are these 'others'? Is there anything you can do to reassure them?

List 2: Impact on you (internal) and impact on others (internal).
What are the inner, psychological consequences – for you and others – of choosing this option? Consider sense of worth, sense of identity, pride, happiness, stress, etc. Who are these 'others'? Can they be reassured?

Advice for squirrels

The good news...

You have several solid options you could quite happily pursue. Plus, detailed research is your thing – you won't have any trouble with the information gathering part of this task. As a naturally careful decision-maker, you're unlikely to make a decision without considering each option properly. Also, you've got plenty of time (you hate being asked to rush important decisions).

The not-so-good news...

Slimming down your list from ten to five isn't your idea of fun. Logic and reasoning will provide the backbone of your strategy – but be careful you don't over-simplify the tasks by isolating factors and ignoring their complex interdependency. There is also the danger of ignoring the emotional impact of different options. A decision that looks good on paper doesn't always work out so well in real life.

Expect to find Task 1...

A bit challenging – you do hate to narrow down your options. By all means design your own weighted charts and checklists to help with your logical decision making (you'll love it!), but don't ignore your emotions completely. To ensure you don't dismiss intuitive reasoning outright, keep your list of 'rejected' jobs to hand in case you realise you have dismissed your 'secret favourite' by mistake.

Make Task 2 work for you by...

Noting down how much you enjoy researching each job. By assigning a score to this for each (1 = not excited or interested, 10 = very excited and interested), you can compare them all at the end.

Don't forget...

During both tasks 1 and 2, nothing is ever set in stone. Whatever stage you get to, you can always return to your shortlist of possible jobs. Even if you end up taking a job that turns out not to be right for you long-term, you can always change your mind.

If you're really struggling...

If your head is spinning and you feel yourself losing your judgement, don't plough on regardless. Instead, give yourself a break and come back to the tasks in a couple of days – or however long it takes to clear your head. Some time away from the tasks will also give your emotional responses a chance to kick in. You're likely to have gone off at least a couple of your options by then...

Task 1 results:

My five favourite jobs are:

1. ....

2. ....

3. ....

4. ....

5. ....

Job search: where to start

No idea where to hunt for information? Try these sites for size...
www.prospects.ac.uk
www.insidecareers.co.uk
www.get.hobsons.co.uk
www.targetjobs.co.uk
www.learndirect-advice.co.uk

And don't forget... If you're struggling to see how your job fits into the big picture, search on regular news sites, like www.bbc.co.uk or www. timesonline.co.uk. If the mists are clearing and you're still interested, find more specialist industry information by searching on Google for your sector's trade journal, business to business (B2B) or industry magazine. Many of these are available online.

Brain turning to cheese before you've even started? Researching new careers can feel like a daunting task – but remembering these *do's and don'ts* should help keep you on course...

☑ **Do** stay emotionally detached until you have all the facts. Don't start making decisions before you really know what the job is. If you struggle, treat your task like a uni project you're gathering information for.

☒ **Don't** be put off by teeny bits of bad news, like 'competition is stiff'. So the best people do the best? It's hardly news that success is based on merit.

☑ **Do** focus on aspects of what you find that interest you, not the stuff that sends you to sleep. There might well be opportunities to specialise in the best bits. That said, do be realistic about the amount of mundane work involved – paperwork, if you're considering the police force, for example.

☑ **Do** keep an eye out for related or 'spin-off' jobs that could also suit you.

☑ **Do** find good sources that are well laid-out and inspiring. Don't spend hours on boring websites or reading uninspiring books. They may be under-selling the job. Find sources that seem to be written by people who are passionate about the work.

☒ **Don't** be afraid to venture off the beaten track. Most likely, researching one job will lead you to stumble across lots of others that are related, and perhaps even better suited to you. It's up to you whether you investigate them immediately or make a note and come back to them – just make sure you don't forget them!

'Gut feeling' – friend or foe?

David Winter, careers adviser at The Careers Group explains, 'Emotions can play an important part in decision making, but much advice on the subject ignores this fact. The effect of emotions can be positive or negative. Excitement can give you extra motivation to overcome difficulties or it can make you impulsive and careless; apprehension can make you more cautious so that you don't make mistakes or it can paralyse you. Your emotional response to particular job options can be very complex, arising from particularly strong values, which may come from childhood experiences, from associations with particular people and events or from attitudes you have picked up from those around you. Sometimes it helps to try and 'unpack' the emotions, see where they come from and check whether they are appropriate or significant.'

TOP TIP

Remember your 'three brilliant people' from day one? Go back to them and ask whether they know anyone who works in the fields you're researching. Can you give them a quick ring to pick their brains for extra information?

A handy questionnaire

You have one hour to investigate the basics of each job. If you're still interested after that, go off and do extra research in your own time.

Stop! Put your pen down, and photocopy this blank page as many times as you need – depending on the number of jobs you're researching.

Part 1 – The basics

Instructions: Use the next 60 minutes to find answers to as many of the following as you can:

Job under the microscope:

....

In a nutshell, the job involves...

....

This job or sector impacts everyday life when...

....

Some of the biggest companies that work in this area are...

....

The buzz in this industry at the moment is about...

....

People love doing this job (or working in this sector) because...

....

Part 2 – The small print

Still interested? Then continue your research in your own time. Use the following questions as a guide:

The most exciting companies working in this sector/doing this job right now... Would I want to work for them?

....

The 'big personalities' in this field are...
Do I find them inspiring?

....

As a graduate, my first job in this field would be as a...

....

If I did this job, a typical day could involve a mix of ...

....

Referring to my results from exercise one (on day one), I can see that this job would suit me because...

....

If I get the job and then decide it isn't for me, I will still have picked up some great transferable skills that can be used in other jobs or sectors. These are...

....

 Teatime task

Looking back at today's research, think about:

- Which job did you most enjoy researching?
- Which sounded the most interesting?
- Which job surprised you the most?
- Which job would you enjoy talking to someone else about?
- Which job do you think would use your talents best?
- Which job do you think you would enjoy the most?

When you've had a chance to mull it over, fill in the following:

My favourite job is...

1. ....

My two reserve jobs are...

2. ....

3. ....

In Chapter 6...
How to find the best jobs for you – whether they're advertised or not.

Part 3:
Next steps

The mists are clearing... time to venture forth!

NOTES

Chapter 6:
The job-hunt

Now you know what you're after, the question is: where is your new job hiding?

One of these statements is true. Which one is it?

1. 'All this year's graduate jobs have already been taken.'
2. 'There are no jobs out there – or at least very few.'
3. 'The best jobs are impossible to get.'

OK – I lied. They're all false.

At any given time of year, whatever the economic climate, there are *masses* of jobs out there that you could a) get, and b) do brilliantly. Yes, even in times when you read about rising unemployment, this is extremely unlikely to affect you directly. You are bright, educated and keen to get stuck in. So filter out those nasty negative voices.

There are always plenty of jobs for people like you.

Why? Because the job market is in a state of constant flux. Employees' lives change all the time – people are always on the move. Workers are forever being promoted, getting poached by competitor companies, going on maternity leave, switching industries, taking sabbaticals, resigning, moving to Australia... It's what people do – their circumstances change and they change jobs. And all the roles that they leave empty will need to be filled – either temporarily or permanently.

Plus, good companies are always looking for good people. If they meet you and really like you but don't have the right role for you then they might create one – or ring you when the situation changes.

What you're after is a job you want, with a company that thinks you'll fit in and work hard for them, for a while at least.

There are loads of ways to find jobs. Bear in mind that the level of success you'll have with each method will vary wildly depending on the sector you're hunting in. Some industries are very traditional and bound by strict regulations about hiring (jobs in government, for example, or the NHS) – so the 'tried and trusted' methods are likely to get you the best results. Other industries are more informal and unstructured like TV and film, so you might find that the 'maverick' methods are the way to go. I recommend reading this whole chapter, no matter which field you're hoping to find your first job in, as sometimes the best approach is to try a combination of both styles.

In the early stages of your job-hunt, try every method. Later, you can ask, 'What's working best?' and 'What isn't working at all?' Do more of the things that work, and ditch the methods that don't.

The five golden rules of job-hunting

1. **Keep an open mind.** By applying for a job, you aren't committing to anything. You aren't deciding if you want to take the job, just if you want to meet the people and find out more about it.
2. **Consider geography**. Know where you want to work – and stick to it. Want to work in London? Then don't apply for jobs in Slough just because you're desperate. Be strong.
3. **Don't play favourites**. It's easy to get your hopes up when you see a promising ad, but getting your heart set on a job at ad stage is like declaring you're in love when you've only seen someone's photo. Besides, focussing too much on one job could make you sloppy with your other applications.
4. **Remember it's a numbers game**. Aim to have at least ten applications on the go at any one time. Keep a log so you can chart and monitor your progress.
5. **Expect to have good days and bad days**. For tips on staying motivated, see Part 4 – Tips and tricks.

Where to look – the tried-and-trusted methods

Newspapers

So it feels a bit old skool, but don't underestimate the number of employers who still rate this type of advertising when they have a role to fill.

Some national newspapers run a job supplement once a week that covers all industries. Others advertise jobs in a specific area or industry on a particular day, for example, the *Media Guardian* on Mondays. Most newspapers will feature the same ads online, but check carefully for the date they were posted. Your chances of getting that job narrow with every day the ad has been live. So when you see something interesting, get on it sharpish.

If you're not familiar with the employer who is advertising a position, use their job ad to gather clues about them. A big ad with a company logo suggests a large company with money to spend. A shorter, simpler ad suggests the employer is on a tighter budget, so expect them to be a small or medium-sized business.

And remember, if you don't see many ads for the industry you want to get into, don't assume there aren't vacancies to be filled. If job ads for your chosen world seem a bit thin on the ground, you'll probably have more luck using alternative job-hunting methods, so read on...

66 I was under-qualified – but it didn't matter

I always assumed you had to tick every box on the job description before you applied, but I was getting desperate so decided it was worth a shot and I applied for a sales job that required experience – even though I blatantly didn't have any. Not expecting to hear back, I was shocked to hear I'd got an interview. When I went in, they asked me to explain the company's product (a security system) to them – and the boss said he was really impressed. It didn't matter that I was inexperienced – he'd taken that into account and could see that I had potential.

Demelza Bowyer, 25

2:1, Modern and Medieval Language, University of Cambridge

The job spec – set in stone?

You've seen a job ad you like. There's just one problem: you're missing a few of the requirements. Is it still worth applying for?

'You're always more likely to get something back from applying than not applying,' says Susie Goldie at The Careers Group. 'Even if you're not right for that particular role, the recruiters might hang on to your details for a more suitable post in the future, so you just never know. Having said that, job applications can be time-consuming, so it's worth weighing up the odds before you start applying for hundreds of jobs you're under-qualified for.

'Some job ads will be clear about what are *must-haves* and what are *nice-to-haves*. Others will list them all together, and it can be difficult to know which is which. As a general rule, skills, qualities or qualifications that are described as "essential" are *must-haves* and have been specified for a reason. For example, if they've listed having a driving license, it's because the job involves an element of travel, and they don't want you taking trains everywhere. On the other hand, the little things tend to be negotiable. For example, there might well be room for manoeuvre with things like your typing speed or your experience of using various computer packages.

'What about the length of experience they're after? At entry level, it's likely they mean what they say. If they want a year's experience, it probably isn't worth applying if you only have three months' experience. Having said that, there might be some flexibility if you're only slightly missing the mark, if, say, you have nine months' experience, particularly if you have other qualities that you feel make up for a shortfall in one area. After all, you have no idea of the quality of the other applicants. If the recruiters are struggling to find someone with the right experience and the right attitude, they might well be willing to bend on experience for a candidate who is keen and committed.

'One final word of advice: if you're slightly under-qualified, don't highlight it in your initial application. If you make it to the interview stage, it's a discussion to have then.'

TOP TIP

Spotted an ad for a job you're confident you could do right now? Recruiting can take employers ages so in some cases it's an inspired move to ring and ask if they need temporary cover in the meantime. If they're snowed under (often the case if a PA has left, for example), they might well say 'Yes please!', giving you a great opportunity to get a foot in the door...

Professional and trade magazines

Most industries have their own journal – a magazine produced specifically for professionals working within that world. For example, the charity world has *Third Sector*, the public relations industry has *PR Week*, healthcare professionals have the *Health Service Journal* and TV and radio have *Broadcast*. If you know which industry you want to get into, it's worth tracking down the relevant journal – available from bigger newsagents or online.

As well as having pages of relevant job ads, trade journals contain pages of news stories and features. Get into the habit of carrying them with you to read on the bus, during your lunch breaks or while waiting for your friends in the pub. You never know when a random news snippet you saw weeks ago could make you sound really clever in an interview.

TOP TIP

If you like the look of a job and the company but the role seems too senior, it's always worth sending the employer your CV anyway, explaining that you don't feel you have the experience for the advertised role – but you'd love to be considered for any slightly more junior vacancies they might have coming up… You never know your luck!

Websites

In theory, the web should be the best place to find a job – after all, it has the biggest potential audience of any medium, right? Well, yes and no.

There are several ways to use the web to find jobs.

1. By using job search engines to look for relevant positions that have been posted by employers. Many of these search engines will also to e-mail you 'job alerts' when new vacancies matching your criteria are posted. Depending on the employer and the industry, the next step could mean being directed to their online application system or e-mailing them your CV and covering letter directly.
2. By surfing the web to find individual company websites that might contain pages called something like 'Careers with us' or 'Want to join our team?', giving details of how to get in touch with them directly. There may not be specific vacancies listed, but a page like this shows they're open to direct approaches from candidates.
3. By uploading your whole CV onto a site that employers pay to search, using relevant keywords. Employers contact candidates directly if they think you'd be a good fit for one of their vacancies.

However, despite technological advances, it's worth remembering that there are still major limitations to using the web to actually land a job:

1. Postings are sometimes very brief – and, without a human contact, it can be difficult to find more information about a vacancy.
2. Websites which allow employers to search uploaded CVs use technology that relies heavily on keywords. For example, if you don't have 'IT' somewhere on your CV, you may not be matched with vacancies that require even the most basic IT skills.

3. It's easy to get the impression that these are the only jobs being advertised – when in fact only a very small percentage of jobs are ever advertised online.

4. Many employers consider the web a bit of a free-for-all. Although they might have access to a higher number of candidates, there's very little sense of quality control. Remember, employers only want to hear from the very best applicants. By their reckoning, if they put an ad in *The Guardian*, they know it's probably going to be answered by a certain type of candidate. Post it on a random job board and the good, the bad and the downright mad will apply – and it costs the employer time and money to sift through the huge number of CVs. Snooty and elitist? Yes. But wouldn't you do the same?

5. When filling in online applications, it can feel like you're sending your carefully crafted answers into the abyss. Did it send? Didn't it send? Applying for a job without any human contact can feel clinical and demoralising.

TOP TIP

Posting your CV online? Be careful about the personal information you include – ID fraudsters could get their hands on it. As a rule of thumb, it's best not to include your date of birth or postal address. Your name, phone number and e-mail address should be sufficient.

Recruitment agencies

These companies work by building up a giant database of strong *candidates* (job-hunters), who they hand-pick to fill vacancies for their *clients* (companies who are looking to recruit). Some of the bigger agencies fill all sorts of jobs across different sectors, but often a recruitment agency will specialise in filling positions in a particular field. So before you sign up, check they work to fill roles in areas you're interested in. Find out by asking them directly and looking at their website and the job boards in their offices. Are these the kind of roles you're after? Usually, it's free to get yourself on their books. You can sign up with as many recruitment agencies as you like.

To get the most out of your recruitment agency, it pays to understand the basics of how they work:

1. Job-hunters like you approach the recruitment agency and sign up to be on their books. Usually, the agency will ask to meet you and discuss the sort of roles you'd like to be put forward for.
2. When a client has a vacancy they want filled, they approach the agency and say, 'If you can find a great person to fill this vacant role for us, we'll give you a fee.' In essence, the client is paying for the agency to do the legwork of finding top-quality candidates and then screening them for their suitability for the vacant role.
3. The agency trawls their database to find the best matched candidates. If you are on the list, they'll call you in for a preliminary, screening interview to discuss your suitability for the job.
4. If the agency feels you're a good fit, they'll arrange for you to be interviewed by the employer.
5. If the employer also likes you and offers you the job, the agency gets a fee. The fee isn't deducted from your new salary, it's usually a one-off payment of between 10 – 25 per cent of the value of your first year's salary, and is an entirely separate agreement between the employer and the agency which doesn't affect your rights in any way.

So far, so sensible. The agency is quids-in, the employer fills their vacancy, and you get a job without having to hunt for it! What's not to love?

When the system works, it's great. But be careful about relying solely on agencies to find you a job. Why?

1. Good agencies are great – bad agencies are shocking. You go through the palaver of signing up, being assessed by the agency and then…? Deafening silence. You never hear from them again. If this happens to you, it's not your fault. It's just that they aren't really working for you, they're working for whatever clients happen to need jobs filled at that time.

2. They sometimes forget about you. Big agencies will have enormous books of candidates – hundreds and hundreds of them. It's in their interest – the bigger their stack of job-hunters, the more likely they are to be able to fill vacancies that present themselves as speedily as possible, thus earning their fee from the employer quickly, with minimum effort. Keep in regular contact with them to make sure you're always at the forefront of their minds.

3. Bad agencies can squish your confidence by telling you that you don't have the right skills and experience, or that there aren't many jobs out there that fit what you're looking for. Often this is total rubbish. Usually the truth is that they don't have any clients who work in the sector you're interested in. Or it could be that companies in that sector don't use recruitment agencies to fill vacancies – they use other methods to find new staff.

Headhunters

Tribal types who want your noggin on a stick? Not quite. Headhunters, also known as 'executive search' agents, are like recruitment consultants, except that they usually approach people already in jobs and try to poach them for their clients. They make it their business to know who are the 'rising stars' in an employer's industry and then find them the very best candidate out there. Although traditionally used more at the senior end of the market (i.e. to find more experienced candidates, for senior roles), more and more graduate head-hunters are appearing. If you get a call from a headhunter, it's because someone – a friend, tutor or colleague – has recommended you. Result!

Being approached by a headhunter is super-flattering, but try not to get too excited. In the early stages of a search, headhunters cast their net wide, and your skills and experience might well not turn out to be right for the role after all. If things don't work out, be polite and thank them for considering you – and it's always worth asking them to bear you in mind for other similar vacancies that arise. Oh, and seize the opportunity to bleed them dry for free advice on your CV, interview technique – and if they know any other companies who are hiring at the moment, who might be a good match for you. It's worth a shot!

Temping

If you bag yourself a temping job and perform well in your role, you may well be asked to stay on. Clearly, this is an effortless way to find a job – after all, you weren't even trying! You might not even have to interview for the role, and even if you do then you've got a head start because the employer already knows and likes you, plus you know exactly what the job involves because you've been doing it for a while already.

If you get on well within the company, there are opportunities for training and swift promotion, the money is decent and the job is pretty reasonable – working on a busy, buzzy reception or as a personal assistant, for example – the offer is worth considering. Could this job make a perfect little first job to tide you over and gain you some valuable transferable experience?

Think carefully, though – especially if the job is low-level admin work, like data-entry, filing or de-stapling. (Yes, all right, this was me. And yes, I was literally *removing the staples from pieces of paper*.) It can be tempting to grab the first job you're offered – plus it's always flattering to be asked – but take care not to sell yourself short if you know you can do a lot better. If you think you'd be bored of the job in under a month (or totally depressed to know you actually worked permanently for that employer) and can afford to stay temping, it's probably worth holding out for another opportunity.

Work experience and internships

Yes, it might mean making tea – for free. But work experience and internships are still the best (and sometimes the *only*) way in to industries like TV, film and fashion. It isn't just about 'paying your dues'. Make a good impression and they'll bear you in mind next time a job comes up.

For more information on work experience and internships, turn to Chapter 8: Alternatives to the job-hunt.

Recruitment fairs

No candyfloss, no helter-skelter – just lots of employers keen to encourage you to apply to work for them. There might not be any goldfish-in-a-bag to be won, but if you know what sort of job you're looking for, recruitment fairs do offer the chance to come eyeball-to-eyeball with potential employers – and can be a good way to get a feel for what a company might be like to work for. They're also a great place to stock up on free pens and stress-balls – most companies give out some kind of gift to get you to remember them.

So how do recruitment fairs work? Well, each employer has paid the organisers a (fairly hefty) fee to have a 'stall' at the fair, knowing that this is a great opportunity to meet top-quality graduates who could come and work for them. Each employer sends along a few members of their staff to chat to graduates about the company and give out free copies of various brochures for you to take away and read. They might also take a copy of your CV or ask you for your contact details so they can get in touch directly when vacancies arise.

Recruitment fairs – do's and don'ts

☑ **Do** find out which companies are booked to attend the recruitment fair before you go. Are they employers you might want to work for? Remember, not all recruitment fairs cover all industries – some are tailored to graduates interested in jobs in a particular sector. Don't go to a financial, consultancy or IT event if you want to get into retail.

☒ **Don't** expect to find small or medium-sized companies at recruitment fairs. Why? Money. With only a small number of roles to fill, they can't justify paying the fee for the stall – it doesn't make financial sense. The big companies will be looking to hire much larger numbers of new recruits annually, so it's worth it for them.

☑ **Do** remember that the companies at the fair are only a teeny, tiny fraction of the companies that will be interested in hiring you. Don't worry if none of them tickles your fancy – there are hundreds of others who just *aren't there.* But, you can find them yourself.

☒ **Don't** go to a recruitment fair expecting to find out what you want to do with your life. In that frame of mind, it's most likely that none of the employers will appeal to you and you'll just end up feeling more depressed. Even worse, you could get suckered into a job you don't really want, all because you're feeling vulnerable and the fair has given you the impression that these are the only jobs that are out there.

☒ **Don't** just bag the freebies and brochures and run. Get chatting to the people running the stalls. Even if they're awful and you decide you'd rather stick pins in your eyes than work for them, you'll learn something.

☒ **Don't** worry that all the other grads (or, worse still, *under*grads) seem super-motivated and uber-experienced. For all you know, they might be weirdos with no social skills! Employers would rather hire interesting people like you.

- ☑ **Do** get stuck in to any relevant employer workshops or presentations that are happening during the day.
- ☒ **Don't** just wander around aimlessly.
- ☒ **Don't** expect to see creative or media companies at recruitment fairs. You might find the odd fashion retailer (like Abercrombie and Fitch), newswire service (like Bloomberg or Reuters) or financial newspaper (like the *Financial Times*), but you won't find TV channels, film production companies or art galleries. Similarly, you're unlikely to spot architects, graphic design agencies or anyone from advertising, events or PR. On the whole, these companies already receive plenty of approaches from good-quality candidates, so simply don't need to spend extra money attending recruitment fairs to meet more. If you want to reach them, you're better off contacting them directly.
- ☑ **Do** dress fairly smartly and bring copies of your CV to give to any employers you'd like to hear from.
- ☒ **Don't** carry a briefcase – it just looks weird. Especially if you have to open it and everyone sees that it's empty apart from a sandwich your mum gave you.

TOP TIP

Companies send their best recruiters to these events, so chatting to their chosen one will give you insight as to what the rest of the company is like. Go with your gut – if their best recruiter is pretty lifeless, move on. If they seem nice and normal, grab some information.

Where to look: the maverick methods...

There are other, less traditional methods of job-hunting. To achieve the best results, do them *as well as* the tried-and-trusted methods above. (Remember, keep as many plates spinning as possible...)

The 'keep 'em peeled' approach

Sometimes, some days, when the stars are aligned and the gods are smiling on you, a brilliant opportunity might just fall into your lap. It could be an overheard conversation, a chance encounter or a mis-dialled phone number... Whatever form your lucky break takes, you only have one responsibility: to grab it with both hands. Don't dither, freeze or wimp out. Good old-fashioned serendipity can be enough to get you a job. Someone up there likes you. Go for it.

To work this tactic successfully, all you've got to do is be on your toes.

Just remember, this strategy is a strictly an add-on plan only! If all you do is *keep 'em peeled*, you'll find this tactic looks remarkably similar to, er, doing nothing and waiting for things to happen. (For more information on why this is a seriously bad plan, see Myth 10, Chapter 2).

66 My customer became my boss

After uni, I took a full-time job at Top Shop. My dream of becoming a fashion journalist wasn't working out and I figured at least I'd be around great clothes – and hopefully get an employee discount! One day, I found myself chatting to a customer who was buying shoes – and she mentioned she was the web editor at *Marie Claire* magazine. Without thinking, I told her how I'd been trying to crack into the industry but hadn't had much luck – and was amazed when she gave me her card and asked for my number! She called me a few weeks later, saying there was an opening for an intern in the online team. I did that for two months – and then they asked me to stay on, on a freelance basis. That was four months ago – and I'm still here. It made me realise that so many opportunities never get advertised. Sometimes just talking to people and seizing random chances is the best way in.

Jennifer McNulty, 24

2:1, Media Studies (Print Journalism), University of Westminster

66 A quick chat lead to a brilliant job

My worst job after uni was working in hospitality, travelling to events and serving fancy sandwiches. But a work colleague there introduced me to a friend of hers who worked for a music PR company and I managed to get a work placement there. I was just running errands and making tea but two days later they offered me a job – incredible, but true! Now, I'm a senior press officer for a regional music PR company – exactly the role I was after!

Nola Kinna, 25

2:1, Drama, University College Winchester

MA TV Production, Falmouth College of Arts 99

The 'under the radar' approach

Similar to the *keep 'em peeled* approach, but this requires you to do some running. You also need to have a bit of faith. For it to work, you have to believe a) that some of the very best jobs are never advertised and b) that the only way to hear about them is through *talking to people*.

Now, if you thought job-hunting was all about ripping adverts out of newspapers and sending in your CV, this more nebulous way of thinking – and job-hunting – can take some getting your head round.

'What is she on about?' you're thinking. 'I'm looking for a job that isn't even advertised? Like that's not going to be a total nightmare…!'

The good news is that this approach is far easier than you think. And minute for minute, it works out as one of the most time effective ways to land yourself a great job.

And the pluses just keep on coming. If you do hear about a secret vacancy this way, you have major advantages in your favour:

1. You have proved that you have the nous to sniff out unadvertised jobs like this.
2. You have a 'way in', because the person who told you about the job provides a connection between you and the prospective employer.

3. You're one of very few people who know about this job – so your chances of getting it are far better than replying to an online posting, or an ad in the paper.
4. Even if the employer is planning to advertise the role, you're at the front of their minds because you found it yourself before it was even advertised.

The *under the radar* approach can be applied to any industry – but is particularly effective in industries where professionals rely on similar skills during their day-to-day work. In other words, in worlds where showing initiative, taking chances, making friends, using connections and, crucially, gaining information through *talking to people* are considered major assets, people will be super-impressed if you used this approach to find work in their company. It's a big winner in journalism, TV, fashion and PR.

Coincidentally, or perhaps not, these are also the worlds which you are unlikely to be able to get into *without* using this approach. If you're trying to get into an industry which apparently 'has no door' (like film or journalism, both notoriously tricky to start out in), the *under the radar* approach might be the best chance you've got.

How does the *under the radar* approach work? In essence, it's all about *talking to people*.

'*Bleurgh* – networking?!'

Stay with me, people. Yes, networking has a monstrous reputation. It conjures up images of pushy job-seekers wearing cheap suits and name-badges and sipping warm white wine at conferences, handing out business cards and asking everyone they know to give them a job. Aggressive mingling – urgh, what could be worse? It's desperate, it's tragic and it's *so* not you.

But there's good news. If that's what networking was *ever* like, it's certainly not like that now. In fact, if you do behave like that, you'll need a whole lot of luck if you're ever going to find employment. No one likes a desperado.

Nope, these days the *under the radar* approach is far softer. The secret of modern networking is simple: find people who work in your field – and be polite, interested and charming. Seriously, that's it.

TOP TIP

What networking organisations operate in your industry? Look for ones that are exclusively aimed at people starting out. (For example, if you're interested in publishing, investigate the Society of Young Publishers.) Their events are often a golden opportunity to boost your knowledge and meet potential employers.

❝ Meeting industry types really paid off

My big break was being invited to represent my uni at the annual New Designers Show – even though, at the time, I'd never even heard of it! Basically, it's a giant, four-day fair where design students showcase their work. Huge companies like Audi, Nike and Dyson come to scout for potential employees. I was amazed when I was approached by a recruiter at Lego, who said he loved my work (a secure backpack), and offered me an interview for a brilliant job which I ended up getting! I'd definitely advise graduates to go to industry events like that, whatever sector you're interested in. You never know who you might meet – or what they might offer you.

Harry Botterill, 23

1:1, Industrial Design and Technology, Loughborough University

How to schmooze

Make a list of everyone you know who works in the industry you're interested in. This can be anyone – your brother's friend, your cousin, your godfather, friends of your parents... If you're interested in a research post or other job that's related directly to your degree, be sure you also include professors and tutors. Get everybody's e-mail address.

Make a list of other people who might know people who work in the industry you're interested in. Phone them to see if they do. Get e-mail addresses.

Send them a charming e-mail introducing yourself, clarifying the personal link between you and them and asking – so politely – for half an hour of their time when you could come and have a chat with them.

Make it clear that this can be any time that is convenient for them. (If they're super-busy, ask them to suggest a time when you could give them a ring to chat instead).

Don't be late for the meeting. Look smart(ish) and bring your CV so you don't have to waste time talking them through your experience. Bring a pen and paper and take notes, jotting down any names, websites and organisations to look up at a later date.

Ask them how they would progress with a job-hunt in this area if they were you? Do they know anyone who you might be of help, i.e. who might consider hiring you? What sort of experience might be valuable to get in the meantime? Don't ask them directly for a job.

Resist the urge to slag off your previous/current employer – no matter how evil they are. You want to look positive and up-beat, not bitter and bitchy.

Ask if they have any other friends in the industry who you could e-mail or speak to – even about work experience or temporary work in the industry. Ask them to let you know if they hear of any jobs that you might apply for – and if they can send you any job ads that come their way.

Forget nothing. Straight after the meeting, write down everything you can remember about the conversation, while it's still fresh in your mind. E-mail them within 12 hours to thank them for their time and say you will keep them posted with how you're getting on.

Keep in touch with your contacts and inform them of your progress, telling them exactly how their information has helped you.

The 'if you don't ask' approach

Got an idea of who you might like to work for, but can't find any job ads for vacancies there? There's nothing to stop you from sending them your CV and a polite covering letter anyway – also known as the 'speculative approach' or 'applying on spec'. Go on, what have you got to lose?

Start by finding the name of someone in the HR department (Human Resources, formerly 'personnel'). They're the people who will know about all the official vacancies. It's also worth contacting people within the department you want to work for, since not all vacancies are advertised and filled by the HR department. (For example, newspapers editors are notorious for ignoring HR completely, recruiting people themselves.)

Tailor your CV and covering letter to that company and post or e-mail it to the correct person. Run them through your skills, explain how much you'd love the opportunity to work for them and politely ask whether they could get in touch with you if any suitable vacancies arise. (If possible, research the exact job titles that would suit your level of experience, to show you understand the company structure and that this isn't just a stab in the dark.) Explain that if they don't have anything at the moment, you're very happy for them to keep your details on file for the future. You'd be surprised – most employers actually *do* hang onto good CVs.

What's the worst that can happen? They say, 'Sorry, we don't have any vacancies at the moment, but we'll hang on to your CV for the future and be in touch if anything opens up.' You say, 'Thank you, that's great.' Disaster? Hardly. Embarrassing? No. And who knows? They might actually call you.

It's worth mentioning here that speculative applications can be particularly effective when targeting smalller companies (who are less likely to advertise vacancies, for cost reasons)

Yes, a big company will give you an impressive, recognisable name on your CV forever. They're likely to invest in formal, organised training, also great for your CV. As part of a batch of grads, you will have plenty of people your age to hang out with. And, if all goes well, there's probably a structured career progression you can expect to follow in the future.

But there are also advantages to working for dinkier companies. A 'small to medium-sized enterprise' (SME) is defined as one with fewer than 250 employees. Some may have as few as three or four!

What are the benefits of working for a dinkier operation?

- A more personal work culture – people will know who you are – you won't just be a face in the crowd.
- Earlier opportunities for responsibility, promotion and career advancements – there's likely to be more flexibility within your role, as jobs are less rigidly defined. Your job should become more tailored to your strengths, so you have to battle less with your weaknesses.
- A more entrepreneurial, less hierarchical environment – working more closely with the bosses, you'll get to see their talent in action, giving you exciting, first-hand experience of how the company works at the top, as well as the bottom, and making you feel more involved.
- Greater scope for contributing your own ideas and seeing them put into action, which is rewarding.
- A simpler, less time-consuming recruitment process. Fewer people will need to 'sign off' on the decision to hire you, which means you'll find out the result much sooner.

Spot SMEs by looking in specialist industry magazines. Don't just read the job ads, read the news stories too. Which small businesses or new companies are winning awards for innovation and creativity? Who has launched the most exciting new service or product this year? If a company is doing well, they're probably a good crowd to work for, plus they're probably looking to expand their staff...

Around a third of SMEs rely on speculative applications from candidates who have researched the industry and the company and decided to contact them directly.

A word about... joining a 'start-up'

'Start ups' – or very new companies – can be hugely exciting to work for. You're joining at a time when anything can happen, and everyone's psyched about the idea of being part of something new.

There are risks involved, though. Depending on how recently the company launched, the team could be as small as three or four people, so it's extra important you 'click' with them, particularly the boss. Also, sadly, there's always a chance that the business will fail (start-ups are often the first casualties of an economic recession, for example). Plus, there's the risk you could be made redundant if times do get tough. Having said that, even established companies make redundancies, so you're never 100 per cent safe. If the worst happens, you'll just have to get a new job.

How do you know if it's worth the risk? Well, the smart thing to do is to get on their website and find out as much as you can about the company before you apply. When did they launch? What clients do they have? Then, if you're invited for an interview, ask questions about how well the company is doing (politely, of course!). Has the company landed any new clients recently? How many staff did they have last year? And now? And scope out your interviewers' body language, do they seem happy and confident? (The very fact that they're recruiting is a good sign – they've obviously got plenty of work on, and money to spend on hiring new staff.) Also ask about the professional backgrounds of the boss or bosses. If they used to work for impressive companies you've heard of, they're likely to be smart cookies, which all bodes well.

66 My luck turned when I targeted smaller companies

I tried looking for work with the large publishing companies – but kept receiving standard rejection letters, signed by the boss's PA. So I changed tack, and started looking for smaller, local publishers instead. I found they were far more receptive – and much nicer, friendlier people.

Sophie Goddard, 23

2:1, English Literature with Language, University of Brighton 99

In Chapter 7...
Running the gauntlet: how to survive the recruitment process.

NOTES

Chapter 7:
Applications and interviews

Anxious about putting yourself out there – or just hoping to wing it? The trick to surviving the recruitment process is understanding it first...

Swing by your local bookshop and you'll discover entire shelves dedicated to subjects like interview techniques and writing the perfect CV or covering letter. If writing and selling yourself aren't your greatest gifts, some of these books might be worth a read.

But you might well not need them. After all, applying for jobs isn't rocket science. Sure, there's a process and a few do's and don'ts, but all you really need is a bit of common sense and some sound advice.

Application forms

Not every job advertised will ask you to fill out an application form, but many do. If you've already tried doing a couple, you'll know that a) they're quite hard work and b) they take ages to do.

This is no accident. Applications are actually *designed* to be tricky, because they're crafted to weed out the weak. Make an application form too quick and easy to fill in and any old chancer will apply. Make it harder and only the truly committed will bother, meaning recruiters have fewer, higher-calibre candidates to select from, which makes their lives easier.

Bearing in mind how much time and work is involved, it pays to select carefully the vacancies you really want to apply for. Filling in an application form is never going to be fun but if you find you're losing the will to live less than half-way through the questions, is something telling you this isn't the role for you? If so, it might be better to use your time applying for a different job, one that actually plays to your strengths.

Assuming that you're filling in an application form for a job you feel you are well matched to and that you genuinely want to do, there are three golden rules.

1. Match your personality to the role

What sort of person is likely to fit this position? Remember, that's the sort of person the recruiter is hunting for. (If you don't have a lot of info about what the role requires, find out more.) Break down that person's qualities – and focus on proving you've got them coming out of your ears. Don't fib

– remember, if you get through to the interview stage, you're likely to be asked to expand on these answers and it will be blatantly obvious that you've been telling porkies. Refer back to the exercises in Chapter 3 for a reminder of your key personality selling-points.

2. Prove your abilities

Saying 'I've got great teamworking skills' won't cut the mustard on most application forms – you're going to have to *demonstrate* your talents by giving real examples. Cast your mind back to times when you were in charge of something or saved a project from disaster. In particular, recruiters go nuts for demonstrations of your leadership abilities. And don't forget, these examples don't need to come just from any work experience you have. If you captained a sports team or directed a play, this is the moment to shout about what a star you were.

3. State your case

Making an application isn't just about giving information. However sparkling your record is, it won't just speak for itself – you'll need to be persuasive. Bigging yourself up might feel cheesy, but employers expect you to make an effort to convince them you're the answer to their prayers. You're presenting a rationale for your application – arguing your case for why they should give you the job. Don't be aggressive, though. 'Smart charm' is a much better weapon. Get this right and you'll be ahead of the competition at the interview stage.

TOP TIP

Apply as soon as you see a job advertised. Applications are often filtered as soon as they start coming in and interviews start long before the final deadline.

The secret to stellar application forms

- If you're being asked to fill in a hard copy, i.e. actually to write on a piece of paper and send it in, photocopy the form several times so you've got something to practise on – and use the copies to draft each answer in full. Don't touch the real thing until you know exactly what you're going to write and that your answers will fit the boxes on the form.

- Crossings-out and messy blobs of correcting fluid are not a good start. It might seem harsh, but making mistakes on an application form could suggest (even subconsciously) that you're the sort of person who will make mistakes in the job.

- If it's an online form, don't be tempted to type straight into the box – it won't be your best effort. Instead, print out a hard copy and go away and think about it.

- Read the small print – and follow the instructions. They want black ink? Give them black ink. They want block capitals? Give them block capitals. Don't think it doesn't really matter. It does. If you can't follow simple instructions like this, what does it say about your attitude in general?

- For each question, ask yourself: 'Why are they asking me this? What do they want me to demonstrate?' They want your response to reveal something about you as a candidate. What is it?

- If a question doesn't apply to you, write 'question not applicable' and a brief (one sentence) explanation as to why, if necessary. Don't ever leave empty boxes. It looks like you missed them out and forgot to come back to them.

- Use positive and specific words to describe your skills rather than vague terms and clichés. ('I'm a team player' and 'I always give it a hundred and ten per cent' will make recruiters groan). Likewise, when detailing your goals, don't just say, 'I want to make a difference' – explain what difference you have made so far and exactly *how* you intend to do more.

- Resist the urge to quote facts about the company back to them. The recruiter already knows them!
- Don't get bogged down with complicated storytelling. The employer doesn't have time for a shaggy dog story – just give them the highlights that will interest them the most.
- Try not to lump companies together with their competitors. Recruiters like to see you know why they are *different* from other companies in their sector.
- By all means go into detail about your skills (giving evidence where you can) – but do make sure they're skills that are *relevant* to the job you're applying for. If they're linked or similar to a skill required for the job, be sure to make this link clear. You don't want an employer to think, 'Why on earth is this applicant telling me this?'
- Online applications are sometimes 'read' by some kind of search tool, which scans your form for certain valued keywords. Take a sensible guess at what they might be for the role you're applying for, and make sure you use them. If it's a technical job, use industry specific terms and keywords that you know will be familiar to the employer, but never use jargon if you're not sure it will be understood.
- Try to avoid starting every sentence with 'I'. No one wants to work with a megalomaniac.
- Stick to word limits and the space given. Unless they say it's OK, never continue your answers on a spare sheet of paper. You'll only be waffling.
- Don't repeat examples. A fresh one is always better.
- Check and double-check that your spelling and grammar is impeccable. Then get a friend to check it too.
- Before you send off the completed form, take a photocopy of it. If the employer wants to meet you, reminding yourself of your answers will help you prepare for the interview. You'll look like a prize wally if you can't remember what you wrote.

TOP TIP

Check your outgoing voicemail message. If employers are likely to phone you to arrange an interview, is your greeting appropriate for a potential employer to hear? If it's you doing your best Homer Simpson impression, change it. You can treat them to that once you've got the job.

If you're worried about application forms, you can buy whole books dedicated to getting them just right. But to be honest, the difference between an OK answer and a brilliant answer isn't rocket science. It just takes a bit of practice to critique your answers as an employer will.

Here's an example of how a few quick changes can really beef up your chances of getting your form out of the *maybe* pile and into the *yes* pile...

The question:

'Give an example of when you generated a better way of doing things that led to improved results.'

An OK answer:

'Last summer, when I was working at the Beach Cafe, I noticed that the amount of custom that we received between 10 a.m. and noon was quite low. I suggested that we offer unlimited tea and coffee refills and a reduced-price brunch to pensioners at that time, as they are people who would normally be seen passing the cafe in the morning. The manager of the shop did not like the idea but decided to give it a try. The scheme was successful and our profits rose considerably. As a result I was given a salary increase for my efforts.'

Interviewer feedback:

'A reasonable answer and good to have used a work experience example. However...

* there is more emphasis on the story than on the skills the candidate employed. Does the applicant understand what skills are being used here?
* *suggested* sounds a bit tentative. *Persuaded* would be better – and tell us exactly how this was done.
* 'profits rose considerably', 'salary increase' – good to mention the financial impact, but it would be even better to give us some figures to back this point up.'

The genius answer:

'Last summer, when I worked at the Beach Cafe, I noticed that the amount of custom we received between 10 a.m. and noon was quite low. I decided to try and rectify this situation. Firstly, I researched the type of person in the area who would be able to come into the cafe at that time. In consultation with the chef, I then devised a suitable menu for these people. I also suggested that we should offer tea and coffee refills to enhance trade further. The manager was unsure whether the scheme would work but after I had discussed it with him in detail and modified my plan after listening to his suggestions, I persuaded him to allow me to trial the scheme. After two weeks our profits had risen by 35 per cent. The manager congratulated me on my success and gave me a 20 per cent pay rise.'

Interviewer feedback:

'A far better answer, less story and more about skills. In particular...

* 'decided' is a much stronger word than 'suggested' – and I liked the reference to the research carried out.
* the applicant clearly understands the skills they were using and they match what we are looking for. A good range of skills are being shown here: *researched, consulted, listened, persuaded...*
* 'persuaded him to allow me to trial the scheme' is excellent. At first the manager is unsure, then he is persuaded. Next, his suggestions are incorporated into the plan and then a compromise is reached between the applicant and the boss.'

Five application form booby-traps – and how to dodge them

'Next time you're asked one of these, stop and think before you answer,' says David Winter, careers adviser at The Careers Group...

The 'why?' question

'Graduate training is expensive for employers,' says David. 'This is them asking themselves, "Is this applicant a good investment?" They want you to demonstrate a thorough understanding of the role, to show that you've thought it through and are likely to stick with it. So, tell them how you got interested, what specific aspects of the role or organisation attract you and why – and what you've done to find out more.'

The communication question

Saying you're 'good with people' or have 'an excellent phone manner' isn't enough. Communication is a vital and complex skill and employers want you to demonstrate every aspect. 'For example, if you're talking about a time when you persuaded someone to do something, don't be afraid to go into serious detail,' says David. 'What preparation had you done for the conversation? How did you choose your moment to approach them? How did you handle their questions and concerns? And don't forget to show you can *listen* as well as talk. Graduates often forget that listening forms a major part of communication.'

The teamwork question

Hold fire – this one isn't about the achievements of a team you were once involved with. Instead, it's about how you *behaved as part of a team*. Subtle difference – big impact, says David. 'The biggest mistake graduates make is to go into great detail about how a group they were part of (say, a sports team or cast of a play) pulled together to achieve a joint goal.' But employers aren't interested in the other members of your team – they aren't the ones applying for the job. *You* are. 'Stick to talking about the part you played in the team. When things went wrong, did you help motivate others? Or did you support weaker members of the group, or even the team leader? If so, tell the employer exactly how.'

The leadership question

Freaking out that you've never chaired a debate or edited the university newspaper? No need – this question isn't asking you to show you're prime minister material. 'You don't need to have had a leadership role to answer this one effectively,' explains David. 'The employer is asking you to demonstrate that you have the various qualities that a good leader needs. You may have demonstrated these qualities even if you've never been designated as "the leader". Aim to give the employer confidence that if you were given a leadership role, you could perform. Can you think of a time when you got a project off the ground, even if you didn't end up running it? Are you good at monitoring a team's progress? Have you been able to coax weaker or shyer members of a team into making a useful contribution?'

The commercial awareness question

If you're going to play with the big boys, you really need to know what you're talking about. The biggest mistake graduates make? 'Not doing enough research,' says David. 'Employers don't expect you to be the world expert on their subject, but they do expect you to have a solid background knowledge of where their company fits into the rest of the industry and to understand how any recent economic, social or political changes might have impacted their work,' says David. In other words, if you're applying to Oxfam, don't just waffle about the charity sector in general or how the world is such a terrible place – and don't assume that nothing has changed since your pre-uni gap year in Tanzania. Make sure your knowledge is bang up to date.

Five steps to a brilliant answer

'Question: In 250 words, explain why you have applied for this role. Offer evidence of your suitability (e.g. courses undertaken, work shadowing, skills, strengths and experiences). Emphasise why you consider yourself to be a strong candidate.'

Step 1

Break it down. For unstructured questions like this, a good rule of thumb is to make three, equally-weighted points. For example, 1) I know I'm good at work like this 2) I know I enjoy work like this and 3) I'm passionate about this company.

Step 2

Organise your evidence. For each point, line up the best facts and examples to back up your case.

Step 3

Draft your answer. Splitting the word count equally, outline the facts and the evidence in proper prose. Stay close-ish to the word count but, for now, don't worry if you go over.

Step 4

Cut it down. Edit your answer to the right length to fit the specified word count. Keep the meaning – but be brutal with flowery language. Don't use five words when one will do.

Step 5

Copy on to the form. Type or carefully hand-write your finished answers onto your 'best' form.

Struggling to describe yourself?

If you can't think of a time when you demonstrated a certain ability, ask a friend for ideas. Often others see us more clearly than we see ourselves.

Alternatively, here are some brilliant adjectives to try for size...

Accurate, adaptable, calm, conscientious, determined, impartial, logical, methodical, patient, persistent, persuasive, decisive, reliable, resilient, resourceful, responsible, self-reliant, sensitive, systematic, tactful, tolerant...

CVs

Despite what you may have read, there's really no such thing as the perfect CV. One that goes straight into one employer's recycling bin could easily end up in another employer's 'interesting' pile. It really is that subjective. What makes a successful CV varies wildly from industry to industry, from company to company – having said that, there are a few points to bear in mind to maximise your chances. Your CV, or résumé, should be short and clear.

'Short' means a maximum of two sides of A4. (Not three, *two*. You're interesting, but you're not that interesting.) 'Clear' means avoiding fancy-pants jargon and abbreviations the employer won't understand as well as making sure the content is sensibly organised and the document is visually appealing. Don't use a titchy font to cram on as much info as you can – instead, go back and make your content more concise, so you can have more calming white space on the page.

What are employers looking for in an application?

'In a word: competence,' says Alistair Leathwood, Managing Director of recruitment consultancy FreshMinds Talent...

'Each employer has their own checklist but at application stage they're really just looking for bright sparks who are capable of commitment. The best way to show this is through facts on your CV, not from waffle on your covering letter. In fact, unless you're applying speculatively (when you'll need to explain why you're contacting that employer out of the blue) it's probably best to assume your covering letter will never be read at all (many recruiters don't have time, especially if they're managing a popular graduate scheme for a big company).

'Ask yourself: "Is my CV strong enough to stand alone?" It should be. Remember, a good degree from a good university shows you can work hard, so you don't need to devote a paragraph in your letter to telling them how 'hard-working' you are. You've already proved it. Include all work experience – whether it's high-powered or not – limit your CV to one page only and keep it neat, simple and readable. Oh, and don't tell your life story – aim to give them a sketch outline of who you are. If the recruiters are interested in learning more, they'll ask in the interview.'

And Alistair has one final piece of advice for hard-copy applications: invest in some decent stationery. 'If you want to make a good impression, do it by printing your application on good quality white paper. The really cheap stuff can look pretty nasty.'

So, how to structure your CV? Well, there are zillions of ways of setting it out, but typically they will contain the following information:

1. Your personal details at the top – including your e-mail address and phone number. Don't take up precious room by putting, 'Name:' 'Address:' 'E-mail:' 'Telephone:' etc. Save space by running it all in together. It's optional to put your age, nationality and gender.

2. A 'career profile' – around four sentences about who you are and what sort of job you want. This is optional – some recruiters say it's essential, others say it's naff. Likewise, some employers love them, some hate them. Others say that new graduates shouldn't bother with them at all – since they don't have enough experience to make it stand up. It's entirely up to you. Done well and you can sound on-the-ball and super-focussed, done badly and you can seem pompous – or just plain weird. If you do decide to write a career profile, avoid clichéd generalisations like 'dynamic, team player'. Instead, be as specific as you can about what makes you a particularly good match for this role. If you've already given this information in your covering letter, it might feel repetitive, but remember that there's no guarantee that your covering letter will even be read if your CV isn't impressive enough.

3. Your employment history (including work experience), which should be listed backwards, i.e. starting with your most recent job – include the dates you worked there, the name of the company and your job title. There are no hard-and-fast rules about how much to include but if you have lots of experience, give the most relevant positions the most room, group similar jobs together to save space and consider losing the oldest items (is that work experience at your dad's office when you were 16 really adding anything?). If you don't have much to work with, don't panic. Just spend extra time making what you *do* have sound as impressive and relevant to the job you're applying for as possible. (See Chapter 2 for tips on bigging up rubbish holiday jobs.) Briefly explain what each role involved, using strong 'action' words (See 'Can you speak CV?') and include any key achievements. Also try and weave in mention of your skills, in sentences such as, 'Won new customers using strong negotiation skills...' Try and use the word 'team' where you can – most employers like to see you can work well with others. If you worked alongside any senior staff, mention it here

– and if the company isn't well-known, explain what it is, including the number of employees, to give a context. Avoid using abbreviations or jargon the recruiter won't understand. Big yourself up – but don't overdo it. You still want to sound likeable.

4. Your academic qualifications (again, listed in reverse) right back to your GCSEs, including the full name of the schools / university / college where you gained the qualifications, plus the dates you studied or graduated. Don't list every GCSE – putting '4 As and 5 Bs, including Maths and English' is fine, or '9 GCSEs at grades A–B, including Maths and English' (Maths and English tend to be the only GCSEs that employers really care about). Be specific about your more recent A-level and degree subjects – they might make good conversation if the application progresses to interview stage. If the work you're applying for will make direct use of your degree, then give full details, highlighting any particularly relevant modules/courses you took and briefly explaining your dissertation if you think it's of interest.

5. Any relevant courses you've taken and additional skills, including any other languages you can speak, which IT packages you can use and your touch-typing speed (if you know it).

6. Extra sections like 'Travel' and 'Other Interests' are optional, but can be a great way to show you are a real human being who has a life beyond work. It's great if you have something decent to put in (like being a trained snowboarding instructor, or having been a Student Union rep or a member of a University sports team) and, if applicable, mention the level of achievement you have reached and any specific things you have done that indicate your commitment. However, if you don't have anything good to put here, don't write rubbish for the sake of it. Employers don't care that you were a member of your university Cheese Society for a term. And whatever you do, don't write 'Going to the cinema' under 'Interests'. It's lame.

7. Generally at the bottom of their CV people just write 'References available on request'. Have some names up your sleeve in case the employer wants to take you up on the offer – preferably two people who can comment on different aspects of you. For example, most recent graduates list one tutor or lecturer, plus an employer. If you can't get one of those, it's fine to have a professional person who knows you in a personal capacity. Close family members aren't the way to go here ('My mum thinks I'm wonderful…') – but aunts, uncles, godparents and family friends are perfect for the job.

TOP TIP

The only real CV no-no is to have a big gap. At best, employers will think you've been sitting on the sofa at home for a year. At worst, they'll think you've been in prison.

Is it ever OK to fib?

When you're getting desperate it's tempting to tell a few white lies in an attempt to fast-track your way to a job. But is it wise to start telling porkies? It's up to you – but most recruitment experts recommend sticking with the truth. Even a harmless lie on your CV can get you into a pickle in an interview – and interviews are stressful enough without trying to remember what you lied about in your application. Also, fibbing to a potential boss isn't a great start to your professional relationship – plus you risk landing a job you're too inexperienced for, which really won't be fun.

66 My white lie came back to haunt me

After graduation, I applied to help run a youth scheme in Australia. I had loads of true stuff on my CV I could talk about but of course the interviewers homed in on the one part I'd 'massaged' slightly, and kept asking about my 'extensive experience' working for Nightline (the confidential phone counselling service for students). It wasn't total fiction... I had worked for Nightline – but only as a trainee for a couple of weeks, before I realised I'd have to go on lots of courses to become a proper counsellor. I managed to blag it and got the job, but always worried I'd be caught out. What was I thinking, lying about voluntary work?! I'd never do it again – it's not worth the stress...

Sharon, 23

(Other details withheld. I don't want her blacklisted!)

A word about... spelling and grammar

You can't take enough care over getting your spelling and grammar right – especially if you plan to send this document out again and again to lots of potential employers. Spell-check it *and* get a wordsmith friend to proof-read it. Yes, even if you're good with words yourself – it's easy to miss something. And typos are *so* not a good look. Just one error can make an employer think 'sloppy'. So don't risk it.

A word about... 'standing out'

Heard stories about the thousands of candidates who apply for every vacancy? Are you desperate for your application to stand out from the sea of competitors? Don't be tempted to try stunts and gimmicks to get noticed. Employers will sniff the whiff of desperation a mile off – ker-azy coloured ink and 'unusual' fonts will get you noticed for all the wrong reasons (black and arial font are fine) and never attach a photo unless specifically requested. Whatever you've heard, have faith that excellent candidates stand out simply because they're excellent – yes, even in the most competitive fields. If you've taken real care over your application, this should be you.

Can you speak CV?

Swap wishy-washy lingo for snappy business-speak – and sound smarter in seconds!

'started' –	launched, championed, spearheaded, pioneered, implemented, set up
'thought up' –	created, initiated, brainstormed
'found' –	sourced, discovered
'sorted out' –	arranged, prepared, improved, increased, chose
'fixed' –	improved, streamlined
'picked' –	selected, chose
'tried out' –	tested, trialled
'made' or 'did' –	achieved, built, produced
'organised' –	co-ordinated, directed, led, decided, planned, prepared, ran
'spoke to' –	liaised, negotiated, addressed.
'told' –	explained, demonstrated, expressed
'looked into –	examined, analysed, measured, evaluated, interpreted, researched
'suggested' –	proposed, recommended, presented
'worked on' –	developed, implemented, produced, contributed, processed
'looked after' –	supervised, trained, handled
'finished' –	achieved, completed, succeeded, won, delivered, gained
'did the money' –	budgeted, raised

TOP TIP

Don't write 'Curriculum Vitae' at the top – it's pretentious and a waste of space. Don't even put 'CV'. The first line should be your name.

Covering letters and e-mails

Some employers will put it straight in the bin, but others will read your covering letter before your CV, so don't just throw any old thing down. E-mails should be written with just as much care – first impressions really do count. Sound friendly but professional. Be interested and enthusiastic but not desperate or goody-goody – no one likes a brown-noser. And whatever you do, spell your addressee's name right.

Other bright ideas:

- Keep it short – three or four short paragraphs is perfect, and ideally a letter should fit onto one side of A4 paper.
- If you're addressing the letter or e-mail to a named person, sign off 'Yours sincerely'. If you've started with 'Dear Sir/Madam', it's 'Yours faithfully'.
- Print it out and check the spelling and grammar. It's easier to spot mistakes on a printout than on-screen, and typos here really are a disaster. Get someone else to read over it (yes, even if you're confident with your English) – when you've been working on a document for ages you can become blind to errors.
- First paragraph: make it clear which job you are applying for and where you saw the job advertised or – if you heard about it through word of mouth – who told you about it. Introduce yourself, for example, 'I graduated in July with a 2:1 in History from Nottingham University.'

- Second paragraph: explain why you are interested in the role and the company, showing you have a solid understanding of both. (Suppress the urge to suck up here; 'Ever since I was little I've always wanted to work for this company' sounds phoney as well as puke-inducing). Avoid the temptation to say you're applying so that you can 'gain some experience'. Sorry to be harsh, but they're not going to give you the job because you want the experience, they're going to give you the job if they think you can be of value to them.
- Third paragraph: tell them why you feel you're a strong candidate in terms of your abilities, experience and personality. Again, use strong, positive language (see 'Can you speak CV'?). If you can, 'signpost' the recruiter towards the high points of your CV. ('As you'll see from my CV...')
- Final paragraph: wrap it up with a corker. Re-state your interest and suitability for the role, express how much you'd love to have the opportunity to meet with the employer in person and finish with a punchy, positive word or phrase like '...in the future'.

 TOP TIP

Don't get careless. If you have a template letter that you adapt for each employer, it's all too easy to make mistakes. Don't write, 'I'd love to work for Virgin Atlantic' and then send the application to British Airways. It sounds basic, but recruiters at every company will tell you this happens a *lot*. Shudder.

Interviews

Anyone who insists interviews are as much a chance for you to check the employer out as for them to scope you out has obviously never been to one. Sorry, but it's all about *them* measuring *you* – at least in the early stages. Only once they love you do you get to decide whether the feeling is mutual.

The good news is this means they will take charge of the conversation – all you have to do is turn up, keep your head and answer each question as well as you can. And, of course, you can suss them out subtly during the interview – just don't be blatant.

Whatever questions they ask you during the interview (which will normally last around 45 minutes), these are the questions they are asking themselves:

'Can this candidate do the job?' Do you have the appropriate qualifications, knowledge, abilities and experience to do what they want you to do? If you don't have all the knowledge yet, does your track record give them good reason to assume you *will* be able to do the job once you've had a bit of training?

'*Will* this candidate do the job?' Do you have the right motivation, commitment and enthusiasm? Are you really keen on this job or would you rather be doing something else? Will you stick with it for a decent length of time or will you get bored quickly and leave? Remember, re-recruiting is time-consuming and expensive for employers.

'Will this candidate fit in?' Will you fit in with the people who work there and with the company culture? Would people enjoy working with you – and would you enjoy working with them?

Interviews: the golden rules

Before...
- ☑ **Do** eat something beforehand even if you're nervous. You don't want to be shouting over your rumbling tum during the interview.
- ☒ **Don't** glug too much water on your way there. Asking for the bathroom the minute you arrive or squirming in your seat throughout the interview are both pretty embarrassing.

[X] **Don't** ask about the dress code, it sounds fussy and old-fashioned. If you're unsure or they haven't said, wear a suit. It's always better to be too smart than too casual.

[✓] **Do** prepare to talk about yourself in an organised and objective way. Re-read the copy of your application form and covering letter, and familiarise yourself with specific examples of your strengths in action and your best qualities.

[✓] **Do** practise your answers – even if it's on your own. You can try role-playing with a friend but this can feel false – and might actually make you more nervous. Instead, try chattering away to yourself, playing the part of the interviewer *and* yourself. That way, if you give a duff answer, you can just start again. (Yes, OK – you'll sound like a moron. But if it boosts your confidence and gets you the job, who cares?)

[✓] **Do** research the company before you go. By all means ask what the job involves on a day-to-day basis, but asking what the company does is not a good look. To make sure you have been thorough enough, prepare yourself to answer the question: 'What do you know about this organisation?' If your answer starts with 'Er…', go back and find out more.

[✓] **Do** sneakily wipe your hand on your skirt or trousers before you shake hands if you're feeling clammy. Who cares if they notice? It's still better than offering a damp palm.

[✓] **Do** ask for water before you start, even if you aren't thirsty. When you start talking, your mouth could turn into the Sahara. Plus, taking a sip can buy you crucial seconds if you get stumped by a tricky question. (Oh, and make sure it's still, even if they offer sparkling too. This is not the moment for hiccups or a surprise-you-while-you're-talking belch).

[X] **Don't** ask for a hot drink, even if it's freezing outside. It'll be too hot to drink at the start of the interview – and then you'll forget about it.

During...

☒ **Don't** say you'd like the job because you want some experience. They're not going to give you the job because you need experience – they're going to give you the job because they think you can be of some value to them. (Plus, saying you want experience highlights the fact that you're inexperienced.)

☑ **Do** be yourself – an *appropriate* version of yourself, of course – but try and let some of the likeable parts of your personality shine through. They're unlikely to hire someone they wouldn't want to work with or sit next to.

☒ **Don't** slag off your old employer or criticise your colleagues. It looks trashy.

☒ **Don't** be afraid to ask for clarification if you don't understand the question. 'I'm sorry, do you mean…?' it's far better than rambling on and then saying, 'Er, sorry, was that what you meant?'

☒ **Don't** slouch, perch, wriggle or be tempted to fold your arms – no matter how defensive you feel (or however nippy the interview room is). Sit comfortably and rest your hands loosely on your lap and use them to gesture or emphasise your points. This shows relaxed confidence.

☑ **Do** go easy on the jokes. I know I said be yourself, but don't overdo it. One of the major things the employer is thinking is, 'Could we put this person in front of a client? Is (s)he professional enough to speak to the Big Boss?' By all means be animated – just lose the clown shoes.

☒ **Don't** ask 'What's the money like?' If you get the job, the salary they offer will depend on your experience. They won't want to even give you a rough estimate because they know that then you'll ask for more if they low-ball you. If it seems like a classy firm, it's likely to be a fair salary – you can haggle later. Likewise, don't be tempted to ask about holiday. It's a reasonable question, but you'll sound like a dosser.

And after...

- ☒ **Don't** leave your coat behind. Having said your goodbyes, it's mortifying to have to creep back in. And you might catch your interviewers picking over the carcass of the interview, which is blush-inducing for everyone.
- ☒ **Don't** mistake a cupboard for the exit. It's dark in there.

What makes a great interviewee?

Be likeable and be yourself, says Alistair Leathwood, Managing Director of recruitment consultancy FreshMinds Talent...

'Yes, interviewers want to see if you've done your homework, but primarily the first meeting is to check you're a good egg. They know from your CV that you're bright enough to do the job – the point of the interview is to test your non-academic skills. The two main questions I think recruiters really ask themselves during interviews are: "Could we put this person in front of a client without feeling nervous?" and "Would I want to work with this person?" – remember, if they give you the job, you'll be one of their colleagues. Even though it's important to fit in, draw the line at trying to be someone you're not. Even if you fool them during the selection process, you'll be a fish out of water once you start the job, which isn't fun – so hold out for an employer you really gel with. The best plan is to be honest about who you are and what you've achieved (which is why it's wise to acknowledge and explain any low points in your CV). Just remember to speak up a bit if you're an introvert – and tone it down a notch if you're a loudmouth.'

TOP TIP

Can't remember what you're good at? Refresh your memory on your personality plus-points by looking back over your answers to the exercises in Chapter 3.

Practice interview questions

As with application forms, there are some subjects that crop up again and again in interviews. The Careers Group reveal the questions best-loved by employers...

The basics
Tell me about yourself.
What are your key strengths and weaknesses?
Tell me something about yourself that I wouldn't know from reading your application.
What do people rely on you for?
When was the last time you surprised yourself?
Tell me about a big mistake you have made.

Your goals
What made you apply for this role?
Where do you see yourself in five years' time?
What are your core values and how do they relate to those of our organisation?
What do you think will be the most challenging aspect of this role?
What is your ideal working environment?

Getting on with others
Give an example of when you had to work with someone who was difficult to get along with. Why was this person difficult? How did you handle them?
Tell me about a task you accomplished as a member of a group which you now believe you could have done better alone.
Why do people like working with you? Why might they not enjoy working with you?
Tell me about a situation where you changed your behaviour to make life easier for someone else.

Tell me about a time when you helped a colleague who had made a mistake. What did you do?

Planning and organising

Describe a situation where a number of things had to be done at the same time. How did you handle it? What was the result?

How do you balance your academic obligations and your outside interests?

Can you tell me about a situation in which you anticipated a problem early on that saved a lot of work later?

Tell me about a situation in which your plans for something went wrong. Why did it happen? What did you do? What could you have done to prevent it?

Describe a decision you have made in which there were a number of variables to take into account?

Thinking things through

Describe a situation in which you had to change the way you approached a problem in order to solve it.

Give an example of when you have had to make recommendations about something based on your analysis of information.

Tell me about a time when your analysis of a situation was incorrect. What happened? What should you have done?

Making tricky decisions

Can you give me an example of a complex decision you have had to make and how you went about it?

Describe a time when you had to make a very quick decision and it went wrong. What did you learn?

If you could go back and change a decision you made in the past, what would it be and why?

Can you give me an example of when you have backed your own judgement against that of other people? What happened? How did you handle it? Has it ever gone wrong?

Have you ever had to make a decision on someone else's behalf? How did you approach it?

Can you tell me about a time when you have had to make a decision with incomplete information?

When the going gets tough

Describe a task that you completed that you didn't enjoy. How did you motivate yourself?

Tell me about something you gave up on. What else could you have done to succeed?

Give me an example of when you delivered more than was expected of you.

Tell me about something, other than your studies, that you have had to work really hard to achieve.

Thinking on your feet

Can you give an example of a situation when you have had to adapt to an unexpected change?

Describe a situation when you have taught yourself a new skill in order to complete a task.

Can you give me an example of when someone criticised your work? How did you respond?

Tell me about when you completed a task without all the resources that you would have ideally needed.

Can you give me an example of when you spotted something important that needed doing without having to be told?

Getting what you want

Describe a time when you achieved a win-win result with someone who had competing needs.

Tell me about when you have persuaded someone to change their mind about something.

What is the most difficult thing you have had to explain to someone? How did you do it?

Can you think of a time when a misunderstanding on your part led to problems?

What is the most challenging presentation you have had to give? What did you do to make it successful?

Impressing the bosses

Tell me about a recent business news story that you found interesting. Why?

What attributes do you have that would instil client confidence? Tell me how you have used them.

Can you give me an example of when you've saved money for an employer?

What do you think will be the most important issues facing this sector in the next five years?

Are there things that our competitors are doing that we should be worried about?

Taking the lead

How do you get the best out of people? Can you give me an example?

Tell me about a time when you found it necessary to make an unpopular decision.

Tell me about a time when you have spotted and utilised other people's talents.

Principles and honesty

What does professionalism mean to you? Can you give me an example of when you put it into practice?

Tell me about a time when you have made an ethical stand that has cost you something.

Tell me about something you have done in which it was important to pay attention to detail over a long period. How did you maintain your accuracy?

Give me an example of when you have spoken out against something which you didn't think was right.

Describe a situation in which a lapse of concentration on your part led to difficulties.

Outside the office

What was the last book you read for pleasure? Tell me why you think I should read it.

What's your favourite film? Why?

If you had to sum up your personality in three words, what would they be? Can you give me examples to demonstrate these attributes?

Tell me about an interest that you outgrew. What happened?

And the ones you won't see coming...

(Most likely to be used if you're interviewing for a role that involves logical thinking and numerical analysis.)

What is the best shape for a manhole cover? Why?

Approximately how many nappies were used in the UK last year?

How many hairs are there on a dog?

How many table tennis balls will fit into a 747 aeroplane?

How many gents' barbers are there in London?

What is the angle between the hands on a watch when the time is 3:45?

How many different ways can you think of to find a needle in a haystack?

TOP TIP

Can't think of a job-related example of when you demonstrated a certain skill? Draw on your personal life instead. If you've sorted out your squabbling flatmates, use this to show your conflict resolution skills.

Five tricky questions to be ready for...

1. 'Tell me about yourself…'

Er, in two minutes? Resist the urge to tell your life story. If you can, clarify what sort of answer the interviewer is looking for, by asking 'Are there any specific areas that you'd prefer me to concentrate on?' If they leave it up to you, you should have a brief summary prepared. Be sure to keep it as current as possible, outlining who and where you are *now*, with reference to any recent relevant experience and major achievements. Don't waffle – keep it brief. You can always ask them later if they would like you to expand on any area.

2. 'What is your greatest weakness?'

Oh lawks, they're testing your self-awareness, and whether you're about to talk yourself out of a job. Above all, avoid the 'I'm a perfectionist' cliché trap. Surprise them by admitting a real weakness, one that doesn't really impact on the job, and then describe how you overcome it by using strengths which *are* relevant to the job. (Clever, no?) For example, refer to overcoming nervousness at public speaking by thorough preparation and organisation.

3. 'Why do you want to work for us?'

If you're terrified you'll blurt out 'I don't – I'm just desperate for a job!', then it pays to be ready for this one. Focus your answer on one or more positive aspects of the company as a whole – especially factors that make them more attractive than their competitors. You could talk about the excellence of the organisation, their size, their training opportunities, their ethical stance… If possible, try to find links between your strengths and values and theirs.

4. 'Why should we recruit you?'

Many a candidate has been wrong-footed by this one – largely because it can sound so confrontational. But remember that all they're really asking you to do is highlight what you can do for them. In other words, what do you bring to their party? Underline again how your abilities, experience, personal qualities and motivation combine to make you a great little package of potential.

4. 'What salary are you looking for?'

Yikes – the money question. Many grads feel uncomfortable talking cash. You don't want to sound greedy but you don't want to get ripped off either. If you've done your homework and feel confident talking numbers, you can say 'My understanding is that the typical salary range for this type of job is [X],000 to [X],000. With my level of experience I would ideally be looking for around [X],000.' If you feel less comfortable, you could simply say that you're happy to negotiate, and see what they suggest.

TOP TIP

Remember *why* manners matter. Making a good first impression isn't just for the interviewer. If you do get the job, you will probably have to make lots of first impressions (with new clients, for example) and the employer wants to make sure you handle these situations with ease.

The off-site interview

An interviewer might casually suggest holding your meeting outside the office, in a coffee shop, say. This is just to screen out crazies who don't know how to behave in public (they can slip through the net if employers have only met them in sterile interview rooms). Conduct the interview as normal, just hold the door for old ladies and be super-polite to the waitress. Only a really stingy interviewer will expect you to pay for your own coffee, but fish out your wallet anyway. When they insist on paying, say something like, 'Are you sure?' and then thank them. Don't overdo it – it's only a couple of quid and they'll claim it on expenses later.

Five smart questions to ask the interviewer

At the end of the meeting, most interviewers will give you an opportunity to ask them questions. You might want to ask about something they mentioned earlier in the interview – good, because it shows you were paying attention – but if not, it's good to have a couple of other questions up your sleeve. Remember, you're going for polite and interested, not bolshy and confrontational. In other words, don't ask why they think their share price is falling or what they plan to do about the bad press they received over the weekend…

1. **The job:** Are you able to give me any more detail on what my responsibilities might involve? Can you tell me how a typical day might be spent? What size team would I be working in?
2. **The company**: Can you give me any idea of how the company is looking to grow or change in the next few years?
3. **Training**: Can you tell me what training is offered? Is this done in-house or by an external organisation?
4. **Career development**: Are you able to tell me more about your career development and appraisal system?
5. **The selection process**: When can I expect to hear whether I have been successful at this stage of the selection process? What will the next stage involve?

66 I turned up unprepared

My most disastrous interview was with one of the big investment banks. The previous day, I'd been at an assessment centre for a grad scheme (which I didn't even end up getting). I intended to study the night before, but hadn't realised I'd be so shattered, so just fell into bed. In a nutshell, I completely bombed at the interview. It was so obvious I had no idea what the company was, or what the role involved. I heard myself stuttering and completely fell apart. It was toe-curling. I learned the hard way that when it comes to interviews, you can't just wing it.

Daniel Davis, 23

2:1, Modern Language (Spanish) and Business Management, University of Manchester 99

66 Feeling ready boosts my confidence

It's easy enough to look good on paper, but in an interview there's nothing to hide behind. That's why preparation is key. Not only will your answers be better, but you'll also feel so much more confident going in, if you've done your homework. It's horrible arriving for an interview and knowing you should have done more research. It's hard to look relaxed when you're a jibbering wreck inside. When you feel prepared, you give a much calmer, more positive impression.

Fiona Ball, 21

2:1, Law, University of Cambridge 99

Going blank in interviews

They've asked a simple question – but your brain has left the building. What now?

'Interviewers will be able to tell if you've gone blank during an interview,' warns Laura Brammar, careers adviser at The Careers Group. Whatever you do, resist the urge to spout rubbish to buy time. 'Keep calm, paraphrase the question back to the interviewer to make sure you understand it. This will give you some time to think. If you're still struggling to come up with a response, ask the interviewer: "Can you give me a couple of moments to collect my thoughts?" By acknowledging what's happened, you're taking control of the situation and asserting yourself – which should also help you calm down and think clearer so you will be able to think of an answer to the question.' And if nothing comes? 'It's perfectly acceptable to ask if you can come back to that question later.'

Other types of interview …and how to handle them!

The panel interview

Don't panic if you find yourself facing three or four people – usually this just means there are lots of people interested in hiring the right person. One may lead the questions, one may only be there to observe and therefore say nothing. Direct your answers to the person who asked the question, but include the others with the occasional glance.

The phone interview

This cost-effective (i.e. cheap as chips) method of early-stages screening is usually just to gather more information and decide whether to invite you for a formal, face-to-face interview. Occasionally the phone call will be unannounced – but usually the recruiter will phone to arrange a suitable time to speak to you at a later date. Prepare for a phone interview as if it were a face-to-face interview. It's also wise to have your application form and CV to hand (you might need to refer to it), and keep a pen, paper and your diary handy in case you need to make notes or make an appointment to come for a face-to-face interview. Oh, and have a big glass of water handy in case your saliva vanishes the minute you start talking.

The stress interview

We've all heard tales about the nightmare scenarios where the interviewer says nothing at all, or simply, 'Impress me' – but so-called stress interviews are very rare. You have two choices – play their game or leave. If in doubt and you feel a situation is unreasonable or humiliating, I say stand up, shake the interviewer's hand, thank them and leave. It might even get you the job.

And what *not* to say in an interview…

'I know everyone says this, but ever since I was little I've wanted to be a receptionist / management consultant…' It's over the top – and no one believes you.

'I should just tell you… I've been in prison.' Even as a joke.

'I've been to so many interviews and that question gets me every time!'

A sure-fire way to blow your chances again...

'I'm a Socialist' – when you mean you like working with people. True story – nerves are a terrible thing…

Dyslexic?

With around one in ten people showing signs of dyslexia (around 4 per cent affected 'seriously') you're definitely not the first dyslexic candidate to apply for a job. Obviously, it's wise to give yourself plenty of time to complete applications and get a wordsmith friend or relative to check your form, covering letter and CV carefully. If your application progresses to the next stage, Vicki McNicol, spokesperson for The British Dyslexia Association, says it's wise to bear the following in mind:

'If and when you tell a recruiter that you're dyslexic is entirely up to you. Matters are improving, but unfortunately many employers remain fairly ignorant about dyslexia, so it pays to be cautious. Do your research and find expert advice to help you make an informed decision.

'If you disclose your dyslexia at interview stage, be prepared to discuss frankly how it affects your work – and how it *doesn't* affect your work. Remember, some employers simply won't understand what being dyslexic means in day-to-day terms, so take the reins and explain it to them clearly and confidently. If you have particular difficulty with certain tasks, it could be wise to mention it – as well as explaining how you overcome these problems.

'Be sure to highlight any ways in which you believe your dyslexia is an asset. For example, are you more innovative than your peers? Are you more creative? Or a better problem-solver?

'In the UK, the updated 1995 Disability Discrimination Act makes it illegal for employers to treat you any less favourably on the grounds of your dyslexia and they must make reasonable adjustments needed for you to perform to the best of your ability, from the recruitment process right through to the end of your employment. This can include finding alternative ways to test your suitability for a role, should the existing methods put you at a disadvantage, providing assistive software or tools, finding a quiet location, or simply giving you extra time to complete selection tasks and tests. (Incidentally, tests should be limited only to those which are strictly relevant to the position.) Just make sure you ask in good time.'

For more information visit **www.bdadyslexia.org.uk**.

Jumping through hoops: assessment centres and other selection tests

You've sent your application, CV and covering letter and they've interviewed you – *surely* the recruiter has all the information they need about you? Not quite – there are a few other things they want to know, plus there's no substitute for seeing you in action.

Nerve-wracking, exhausting and sometimes downright humiliating, these mini-assault courses are designed for the amusement of recruiters who've come over a bit Alan Sugar. Depending on the company, an assessment day might be straightforward or littered with banana skins for you to slip on. Be yourself and remember to be nice to the other candidates, even if they're dopey and you fear they're dragging you down. Have faith that your brilliance will merely be amplified by their stupidity. Employers are rarely looking for people who shout over others – so being seen to be a bully is not a good look.

What are assessment centres all about?

'Getting a sneak preview,' says Alistair Leathwood, Managing Director of recruitment consultancy FreshMinds Talent...

'Assessment centres give employers a chance to road-test you, to see how you might get on in your first couple of years in the role. The tasks you're given might seem random, but the recruiters are actually testing the sort of skills you'll be using all the time if you get the job. Typically, they want to check that you can handle large amounts of information, organise your time, present ideas and work well with other people. Don't worry if you mess up a bit – your presentation doesn't have to be dazzling and your group task doesn't have to be perfect. Recruiters just want to see that you have the basics – and a bit of potential.'

❝ I survived an assessment centre

In a group of six, I was asked to lead a discussion. I wasn't nervous at all, but the task was harder than I expected. Our group was such a mix of people – one stayed completely silent, while another one kept shouting over me and wanting to be the centre of attention. He was really winding me up but I kept my cool and got through to the next stage. I think the best thing to remember is that you have to treat the other candidates as though you're a team as opposed to competition. The assessors are trained to see how you interact with other people. Being the loudest doesn't mean you're the best.

Julia Edwards, 22
2:1, European Studies, Durham University ❞

Group exercises

Why? To demonstrate your ability to work as part of a team.

What? In a team of four to eight peers, you're given group tasks to complete. These could be anything from discussing and reaching a conclusion about a current affairs topic (so make sure you're on top of this week's news stories), to being asked to build a bridge with only paper and rubber bands.

Gold stars awarded for: Turn-taking, negotiation and diplomacy, analytical and logical reasoning, clear self-expression, lateral thinking, encouraging contributions from quieter group members.

Points deducted for: Interrupting, dominating, shouting others down, getting bogged down with the details, 'competing' with your fellow team members (you'll be assessed individually on merit, so don't worry about being the best) and obsessing about the outcome (remember, it's the process – how you work together – that's most important).

If you only remember one thing... Always make sure you say *something*. Even if your group is successful, assessors can't mark you if you didn't contribute anything. It doesn't matter if your ideas aren't all startlingly brilliant – just be sure to throw your hat into the ring.

Oral presentations

Why? To show off your research and presentation skills.

What? Either in advance or on the day, you're given a topic on which to prepare and deliver a presentation. The subject might be anything: yourself, one of your interests (from your CV), a current news story or an issue that affects the company.

Gold stars awarded for: Summarising or outlining your aims before you start, 'signposting' as you go along (so your audience can follow a clear progression), brief, bullet-point slides, sticking to your time limit, finding a good pace, looking relaxed and charming but also professional, recovering from disaster if something goes wrong (say, if your laptop dies mid-way through).

Points deducted for: Overwhelming your audience with facts and figures, trying to squeeze too much in, cramming too much onto slides or Powerpoint pages, staying glued to your notes, swaying or developing other distracting tics as you speak.

If you only remember one thing... Keep it simple. Your content should be clearly organised and pitched at the right level. It's better to cover too little than too much.

Written exercises

Why? To prove you can analyse information and communicate clearly in writing.

What? You're given a mass of information and asked to write a report or recommendation (usually a persuasive document of some kind) based on your findings. This could be anything from writing a press release on the company's latest product to an assessment of the pros and cons of the company relocating to China. Or it might have nothing to do with the company at all.

Gold stars awarded for: Identifying the key points in a sea of information, constructing a solid argument using the evidence you have, perfect spelling and grammar.

Points deducted for: Getting bogged down with 'red herrings' (it's possible not all the information will be relevant), a sloppy written style, failing to reach a conclusion (fence-sitters can look indecisive).

If you only remember one thing... There is unlikely to be only one right answer. What's important is how you analyse the problem and how clearly you argue your case.

In- and e-tray exercises

Why? To prove you can organise and prioritise day-to-day tasks effectively.

What? One or more 'sorting' tasks, within a time limit. Often this is a 'Monday morning' to-do list, consisting of: e-mails to act on, phone messages to reply to, internal memos to action and other little jobs that need to be done. Which should you do now? Which can you delegate? Which can you postpone?

Gold stars for: Showing clear reasoning for *why* you have prioritised certain actions and postponed others, spotting when items reveal the existence of other 'colleagues' who you might be able to delegate tasks to.

Points deducted for: Prioritising trivial but urgent matters above more important but less urgent tasks.

If you only remember one thing... Don't panic. Remember, the task is only hypothetical, and as long as you can explain *why* you've arranged the tasks as you have, you should be on solid ground.

Aptitude tests

Why? To assess your abilities by looking at your skills and potential, rather than your knowledge. They can also give employers clues about your work style, your ability to deal with your own and others' emotions, your motivations and determination, your general outlook and how you might relate to other people.

What? Multiple choice questionnaires designed to assess your numerical, cognitive, diagrammatical and verbal skills – and your personality, too. Sometimes you can complete the test online at home, other times you'll have to go into the employer's office. The numerical, cognitive, diagrammatical and verbal reasoning questions do have right and wrong answers and there is a time limit – but the good news is that you can improve your performance by practising in advance (by buying books of practice questions, or visiting your careers centre – and some people even swear that brain-training computer games can speed up your response times). Don't panic if the questions seem to be getting harder and harder – the test is probably designed this way. The personality tests do not have right and wrong answers and usually there is no time limit. Instead, you go through giving your 'first reaction' to each question. Later, your answers are scored to indicate your 'personality type'.

Gold stars for: Being both quick and accurate, keeping calm (think 'studied urgency'), trying your best on each question but moving on swiftly if you get stuck. For the personality tests, be yourself and tell the truth.

Points deducted for: Checking each answer thoroughly (you won't have time), spending too long on one question, wild guessing (read the instructions – sometimes wrong answers will count against you). In the personality tests, don't try and predict how they want you to answer – your responses will be inconsistent and they might just think you're weird.

If you only remember one thing... It really is worth practising – especially if your degree was an essay subject and you aren't used to being tested like this. For the personality tests, remember that each personality type brings different strengths and weaknesses to the party. Don't try and hide who you are. After all, you want a job that suits your personality, not one where you have to spend all day pretending to be something you're not.

66 Expect the unexpected!

When I went to an assessment day for a recruitment company, ten of us had to sit around a table and list, in order of importance, the fifteen things we'd take with us to the moon if we were astronauts. What?!

Steve Meek, 23

1:1, Natural Sciences (with Physics and Maths), Durham University

MA Business Management (distinction) 99

Offers

Been offered a job? Congratulations!

But what should you do? Snap their hand off – or haggle for a better deal?

'As a general rule, if you're happy with the offer then accept it,' says Alistair Leathwood, Managing Director of recruitment consultancy FreshMinds Talent. 'Entry level salaries tend to be fair.'

However, if you sense you're being low-balled or are determined to squeeze another couple of grand out of them, then there are things you can do. 'Just tread carefully,' warns Alistair. 'You don't want to destroy the goodwill before you've even started – and remember, offers can be withdrawn.'

Still determined to play hardball, or have questions about the small print? Alistair shares his wisdom on navigating the offer stage…

- ☑ **Do** control your ego if you decide to haggle over money. 'It's a mistake for graduates to go into negotiations with expectations. The salary they've offered you is based on what they feel you are worth to them.'
- ☑ **Do** be honest about your situation. 'If you need more money for a specific reason, such as relocation or to accommodate travel then this can be a starting point for negotiation.'
- ☑ **Do** keep requests modest. 'You might be able to haggle for a small increase in salary, but look greedy and you risk frustrating

your future employers before you've even started. Worst-case scenario: they could even withdraw their offer.'

- ☒ **Don't** play employers off against each other. 'They're looking for graduates who are committed to the cause and not their wallets.'
- ☑ **Do** ask about employer's contributions in to a company pension scheme. 'Boring, I know – but some employers match employees' contributions, either in part or in full. In other words, whatever you decide to set aside every month, they might put the same amount in too. It could be quite a bit of free money.'
- ☑ **Do** look out for 'soft benefits'. 'Do they finish early on a Friday? Or let you work from home one day a fortnight?'
- ☑ **Do** declare up front any holidays you have booked. 'They won't mind now, but if you wait until you start they may not be so happy.'
- ☒ **Don't** delay your start date for the sake of it. 'If you've got nothing better to do, get stuck in to the role as soon as they'll have you.'
- ☑ **Do** tell the truth if you're waiting on another offer. Employers don't like game-playing, but if you're genuinely waiting to hear, just ask for more time and modestly let them know why.
- ☑ **Do** be firm. HR representatives can by quite pushy, but don't let them bully you around. If you need more time, take more time.
- ☒ **Don't** accept the job unless you're sure. If you want to find out more, ask if you can visit the office and chat to a few of the current members of staff, or attend after work drinks or a social event.

Handling rejection

What do you mean they don't want you? Curses!

Being knocked back can feel deeply personal – particularly if you met and liked the people during interview and felt it went well. Unfortunately, being turned down is something most job-hunters will have to face.

'*But why don't they want me*?!' you wail. Not to be harsh, but there are lots of reasons why you may have received the thin letter (or the short e-mail):

* Someone else was just a little bit better. You can't do anything about the competition.
* You had the right skills – but not enough experience. You can get more.
* You had the right experience – but not enough skills. You can learn more.
* They thought you had potential but they need someone who can hit the ground running. You're good, but you just need to find an employer who will train you a bit.
* You gave a couple of duff answers in your interview. Big deal. You'll be ready next time.
* They thought you were over-qualified – and would be bored in a few months and leave. They were probably right.
* They didn't think you'd enjoy the job. They were probably right.
* They didn't really believe you wanted the job. Perhaps they sensed you just wanted *a* job, not necessarily *that* job.
* They are fools and can't recognise potential when it's staring them in the face. Would you really want to work for people like that?

66 I'm getting better at coping with knock-backs

Given the number of positions I apply for, it's inevitable I'm going to get a fair few letters back saying, 'Thanks, but no thanks.' Now, I only find it tough when several rejection letters come in the same week – especially if two arrive on the same day. But now, instead of dwelling on it for days, I allow myself a 'pity-session' when I do some serious wallowing. After that, it's straight back to searching the job boards. The best way to feel better about being turned down is to get straight back on the computer and fire off another five applications...

Sophie Goddard, 23

2:1, English Literature with Language, University of Brighton

Ouch – why does rejection hurt so much?

Gael Lindenfield, psychotherapist and author of *Bouncing Back From Heartbreak*, explains and suggests ways to move on…

'We've all been there – being turned down for a job you were keen on is really disappointing. Graduates tend to be very tough on themselves a) for failing and b) for getting 'carried away' and imagining themselves in the job before they'd been offered it. But you shouldn't scold yourself for making an emotional connection with a job before you've got it. You need to feel something in those early stages in order to be able to give it your best shot.

'Not only is it OK to feel upset, it's actually *important* that you do. The first step to moving on from pain is to "nurse the emotional wound". Talk about how you feel with someone you trust, who will allow you to feel disappointed for a bit, before they set about cheering you up. The worst thing you can do is suppress your emotions. Resist the temptation to pretend you never wanted the job anyway, or you weren't really trying. If you switch off one set of feelings, you're in danger of squashing other feelings too. And you need to be able to feel. It's your capacity to do so that will help you pick yourself up later on.

'Once you have accepted your disappointment, you might find it helpful to remind yourself of others who have failed – and then gone on to spectacular success. [See Famous failures]. When you're feeling strong enough, it's also wise to try and get some feedback on why you didn't get the job. Breaking down how much of it was actually your fault can help. For example, discovering that another candidate simply had more experience can remind you that the rejection isn't really as personal as it seems. Finally, as soon as you feel up to it, get stuck into applying for other jobs. Who knows? You might even get one of them…'

Really gutted about one particular job? Visit **www.gaellindenfield.com** for more detailed wisdom on how to put it behind you.

Wise words

'Failure is simply the opportunity to begin again, this time more intelligently.'
> Henry Ford (inventor and founder of the Ford Motor Company)

'You may not realise it when it happens, but a kick in the teeth may be the best thing in the world for you.'
> Walt Disney (who went bankrupt – several times)

'I have not failed. I have just found 10,000 ways that don't work.'
> Thomas Edison (who invented the light bulb – eventually)

Famous failures

- Napoleon Bonaparte applied for a position on a naval expedition to the Pacific Ocean, but wasn't selected for the voyage.
- *Friends* actress Lisa Kudrow failed her first audition for an improvisational theatre group.
- James Joyce's first book was rejected by 22 publishers.
- Tom Jones' first single bombed.
- Jessica Simpson auditioned to be a cast member on *The New Mickey Mouse Club* but was rejected.
- Arnold Schwarzenegger missed out on the lead role in the *Incredible Hulk* TV series. Apparently he was too short and skinny.

Asking for feedback

If you didn't want the job anyway, or didn't like the people, you might just want to draw a line under it and forget it. But if you really don't know what went wrong and can face asking for feedback, it's often worthwhile.

Few of us can face picking up the phone and asking why we were rejected, so e-mail is often a more attractive option. The following is a good example of how to ask for feedback.

Dear ...,

Thank you for your letter. I was disappointed to hear that you have decided not to progress with my application but of course completely understand that you feel I was not right for the position. However, if you have the time, I would very much appreciate some feedback on my application, so that I can take your thoughts into account as I continue with my job search.

With many thanks,
Yours sincerely,

....

66 I felt better about rejection after calling for feedback

After sending off about one hundred job applications and receiving an unimpressive five replies – all rejections – I decided to phone the companies and ask where I had gone wrong. Asking why I'd missed out was pretty cringe-worthy, but it was a really valuable exercise. They all said the same thing, that I needed more experience, whether it was paid or voluntary. I had to get the hours in the industry. I'm so glad I bit the bullet and rang. Knowing I'd been turned down for a simple reason like that made it all feel less personal. Plus, now I knew what I needed to do to boost my chances with the next set of applications.

Jane Hewitt, 24
1:1, Sports Therapy, University of Bedfordshire

Back to the drawing board

No joy? If you aren't being interviewed or can't get any useful feedback from recruiters, it could be a sign that you need to go back to the drawing board and re-assess your approach. If it's not happening but you can't work out why, ask yourself the following questions:

Do I need to cast my net wider? It could simply be that you're not applying for enough jobs, or meeting up with enough contacts. Is it possible you're spending too long on each application form, or wasting hours tinkering with your CV when it's already great? Use your time more productively by increasing the number of 'live leads' to follow up. Remember, if you're applying for vacancies you should have between five and ten on the go at any one time. Don't be sentimental – if you haven't heard back after three weeks, consider that application dead.

Am I targeting the wrong employers? Go back – are you sure they all do exactly what you think they do? Do you fully understand the nature of the advertised jobs? Make sure you aren't selling yourself for a job that isn't what you think it is. Is your application badly presented? Sloppy spelling and grammar on your CV really is enough to put off most employers. It's the job-hunt equivalent of having spinach in your teeth and wondering why no one wants to snog you.

Am I applying at the wrong time? If you're approaching employers speculatively, it's just a risk you take. Some companies have strict rules about when in the calendar year they recruit – and when they just don't.

Do I meet the job requirements? Sometimes the job specification (or 'job spec') will have some built-in flexibility – and exceeding requirements in one area can make up for a shortfall in another area. But sometimes they really mean what they say.

Do I need to change my approach? Different methods succeed in different industries. If the ones you're using aren't working, change tack. For example, if you're only applying for advertised vacancies, it could be time to try the 'under the radar' or 'if you don't ask' approach (see Chapter 6).

Am I tailoring my applications well enough for each job? Don't assume one size fits all. Take the time to research the company properly, and show that you understand enough about the business to be genuinely interested in the role. Employers can often tell when a candidate is adopting a 'scatter-gun' approach (i.e. dashing off applications for everything and anything, sending almost identical applications to every job). Re-read the applications you have sent. Be honest – would *you* employ you? If not, it's a better use of your time to cut the number of jobs you apply for and take greater care to tailor each application to that particular job.

In Chapter 8...
Find out what employers think of graduates who do work experience, go travelling or pursue further study.

Chapter 8:
Alternatives to the job-hunt

Finished uni – but not quite ready for the world of work? If you're feeling 'in-betweeny', you might already be considering work experience, further study, or going travelling...

Things are definitely looking up. You've got a clearer idea of what sort of work you might be good at and how to find your first job in that field. But is something still niggling you? Do you feel like you've missed a step?

You're not alone. Lots of grads find that, despite having an idea of what they might want to do, there's a nagging voice in the back of their mind telling them something is somehow *missing* before they can start their job-hunt.

See if these sound like you...

- Would you like to find out more about what it feels like to actually *do* a job, before you apply for it? Are people in the field you're interested in telling you that you need more experience before you can even apply for first jobs in that world?
- Are you getting a sense that you're not quite done with academia? Are you drawn to the idea of further academic study?
- Are you itching to go travelling? Does this feel like the right moment to just go?

While I don't advise stalling for the sake of it (in other words, killing time just because you're scared of facing your future head-on) there are definitely some circumstances in which it's OK – a good idea, even – to put that hunt for your first job on pause for a bit. This chapter is designed to help you recognise whether taking time out to do work experience, pursue further study or go travelling might be a sensible move for you.

Work experience

Do the words 'work experience' fill your heart with gloom? Does your mind race back to long teenage summers spent filing and clock-watching at your dad's office? OK, so maybe it was only a week, but it felt like months. And those sad little lunch breaks you spent sitting alone in a coffee shop, munching an egg mayo sandwich because it was the cheapest filling they had?

Or perhaps work experience, now sometimes called an internship or work placement, makes you think of all your smug super-focussed peers, who got cracking on their work experience long before their finals, knowing it would boost their chances of stepping straight into that first job the minute they left uni.

If you think you've grown out of interning, then think again. They aren't just for students; graduates take placements too and for all sorts of reasons. If you're not sure what you want to do, or have an idea but don't want to commit, then you are a perfect candidate for doing an internship. Not because you love doing all the junior jobs or being paid a modest (or non-existent) sum, but because they can serve as brilliant stop-gaps for people like you. They can be a fantastic way to test out whether or not you think you might enjoy a particular role or industry. Work experience and internships give you a risk-free chance to dip your toe in the water...

'I'm only doing it because I have to'

As much as I wish you were considering work experience just for the sheer joy of it, I'm a realist. I know it's far more likely you're considering work experience because you've been told you should by people who seem to know their onions. If this is you, you're probably feeing fairly resentful about the whole thing already. The news that employers are unlikely even to consider you for a permanent paid role without some junior experience under your belt (either paid or unpaid) probably came as a bit of a body-blow. When you've spent the last three or four years being told how clever you are, being told to start at the bottom – the *very* bottom – along with everyone else can feel pretty humiliating. But don't despair – there's good news. You needn't feel resentful. Work experience and internships aren't merely a shame-inducing formality. Instead, if you can shift your thinking and see it as a fantastic, commitment-free opportunity, you'll find the whole thing much more interesting – and much more fun.

66 Work experience proves you're serious

When I left uni I was keen to get a politics-related job, but I kept getting rejected for permanent roles on the grounds that I didn't have enough experience. I looked into unpaid placements (I'm lucky that I was living at home and my parents could support me) and a small policy and performance company asked me to help out with research. The role was unpaid, but it turned out to be the perfect thing for me. A few months later I spotted an ad for an admin job at a social research office and this time I felt far more confident applying. My experience gave me lots to talk about in the interview and they gave me a one-month trial – which turned into a permanent job! Work experience isn't just 'paying your dues'. Employers see it as proof that you're serious about getting into the industry.

Bola Giwa, 22
2:1, Politics and Business, University of Greenwich 99

66 Work experience helped me rule out what I *don't* want

The summer after I graduated I took an internship at a commercial law firm, like many of my friends. (In our final year, we were bombarded by the big employers.) But I absolutely hated it. I panicked. Internships offer a straightforward career path – why couldn't I make life easy and enjoy it? But it just wasn't for me. I viewed the whole thing as a huge waste of time until I realised: at least now I'd ruled out what I *didn't* want to do! Plus, I'd gained some good office experience. I don't regret taking that internship at all. It taught me not to stress so much about making so-called 'mistakes'. I have plenty of time to try out different jobs and see which suits me best.

Megan Tierney, 21
2:1, Geography, University of Cambridge 99

" I'm juggling paid jobs and work experience

I've been in full time unpaid journalism internships since I left uni. I could ask my parents for money, but I'd rather fund my placement myself, since I chose this path for myself. So, three days a week I do bar work from 9 p.m. to 3 a.m. – and I also work on Saturdays. I know I could stop all this madness by applying for a paid admin job, which I'm sure I wouldn't hate, but I don't want to settle.

Olivia Marks, 21
2:1, Cultural Studies, University of Leeds

The upsides...

When you're doing it for the right reasons, work experience – whether paid or unpaid – can be a brilliant opportunity, and far more valuable than any placement you did at school. You're older, wiser and can bring a lot more to the party, plus there's a lot more in it for you now. An internship is not only a genius addition to your CV – it will also boost your confidence and give you a real flavour of what it might be like to work in a particular job or industry.

And that's not all. Here's what else a work experience placement or internship can do for you...

- ...give you a risk-free taster of what it's like to have a certain job or work in a certain industry. You're unlikely to be given any real responsibility during a work experience placement – so hopefully even if you slip up it won't be a disaster!
- ...give you an idea of what the working environment in your chosen sector is like. It's an opportunity to think about what sort of working environments you are comfortable – or uncomfortable – in. What sort of people do you work well with

– and less well? This is all information that will help you decide what to do next.

- …introduce you to people who might be able to give you job in the future, or tip you off when a position at another company becomes available.

While one short work experience placement is unlikely to result in a proper job with that company, it could mean that you're invited back for casual paid work, which could then lead to a permanent job.

It shows commitment to this role or industry – you aren't about to change your mind and flit off, leaving the employer in the lurch once they've invested in training you up.

It provides you with a basic knowledge of what is involved – you're unlikely to be surprised by the role, or do something weird or maverick when given a task.

It shows potential employers that you possess humility – through acknowledging you have a lot to learn. (Arrogance is a major turn-off to most employers.)

The downsides...

Depending on the sector, work experience and internships may not pay handsomely – you might well find yourself working for peanuts, or nothing at all. It's also worth remembering that, unfortunately, there is no guarantee of a job at the end of a placement, so it is a bit of a gamble. You're also going to have to learn to adopt a sunny attitude, even if, deep down, you're seething at having to do such menial tasks when you're capable of doing so much more. If you turn up with a face like thunder, you might as well not bother – since you won't be impressing anyone.

Why do employers rate work experience so highly?

'It proves you're serious,' says Alistair Leathwood, Managing Director of recruitment consultancy FreshMinds Talent...

'From an employer's perspective, any work experience is good experience – and if it's even slightly relevant, that's a bonus. Many graduates think experience is just a box that employers need to tick. Not true. Employers will take the fact that you've held down a job (or stuck with an internship) as evidence that you make a good employee. To them, the more work you've done, the more likely it is that you are reliable, honest and hardworking. It also suggests that you can handle professional situations appropriately – that you can adapt your behaviour to settings outside the university common room or the pub. If your work experience is relevant to the job you're applying for, you probably have a serious edge on the competition. Your commitment to the field proves a genuine enthusiasm for the work. You aren't just saying you're keen – you're *showing* them.'

Work experience – your questions answered

Q: Is there a difference between work experience and an internship?

A: Not usually, an internship just sounds better. The word is actually an American import – originally used to describe a junior assistant working in politics. Whatever a company calls its most junior placement, it's a good idea to know what to expect, so (politely) find out up front what you'll be doing, what training and support you will get, how long the placement will be for, and what kind of pay you'll receive. A placement can be anything from a week long to several months, paid or unpaid, formal (you'll have a structured programme) or casual (they'll ask you to do whatever needs doing). You might have to go through a formal selection process, or you might not. What sort of work you're given will depend on the company, as will the chances they'll offer you a job at the end of the placement.

Q: I'm picking up the boss's dry cleaning – can this be right?

A: Some industries (such as the media) are renowned for testing their interns' commitment by getting them to do all the really menial stuff. As a rule of thumb, you shouldn't spend all day every day running personal errands for the boss. But yes, you might be asked to do some pretty rubbish stuff during your placement. Often, the worst jobs will come your way on your first day of work experience – as a way to test your staying power. Take on these tasks with a smile, do them properly and efficiently and you can probably expect to be given better stuff to do within a couple of days.

Q: I'm deep in debt, but finding that the industry I'm interested in doesn't pay work experience students. Do they seriously expect me to work for nothing?

A: I'm afraid so. Clearly this is particularly tricky for grads whose parents can't afford to tide them over. But there are ways around it – regardless of your financial circumstances. If you can't (or don't want to) ask your parents to help you financially, you might have to delay taking a placement until you've saved up some cash to fund your living expenses while you're doing it. Alternatively, you can get organised. Book in weeks of work experience in advance, and temp in between placements. Or you could work evenings or weekends for extra money. Remember: it's not forever.

Work experience – your rights

As an intern, where do you stand in the eyes of the law? Heather Collier, Manager of the National Council of Work Experience, explains...

'If you take a paid work experience placement, your legal position is fairly clear-cut. Your employer has the same obligations towards you as they would to any other employee. For example, you're entitled to holiday pay, sick pay and training.

'However, when it comes to unpaid work experience, the rules are less clear. Strictly speaking, the law says that unpaid work experience is only allowed when a student is doing it as part of a course or the placement is with a charity or the placement is work shadowing (i.e. the employee is just observing). In all other cases, workers should receive at least the national minimum wage. There are clearly several strong arguments for this. If an unpaid worker is doing work that a paid worker would otherwise be doing, then that work should be paid. (Incidentally, a worker does not have the right to waive this wage – that's seen as undermining the law.) Another argument is that if a worker is expected to attend certain hours and has certain responsibilities, that forms the basis of a 'contract', even if it's never written down in a formal document. Again, it follows that any such job should be paid.

'In practice, of course, these laws are difficult and expensive to police – and there are currently no resources allocated to checking that employers abide by the rules. As a result, it's well known that some industries – particularly the media – persist in taking unpaid workers in work experience placements. Taking this into account, the Department of Trade and Industry and HM Customs has published a set of guidelines for the media industry (an undertaking co-ordinated by Skillset, the sector skills council for the media industry), at the industry's own request. Although these guidelines were originally drawn up with the media industry in mind, they should be followed by employers in any sector who want a work experience placement student – but don't want to exploit them.

'The guidelines include several reasonable requests for employers to abide by. For example, it's stated that where employers insist on running unpaid placements, these should last no longer than four weeks. They should also involve no more than a 40-hour week, a worker should have an appointed supervisor during their placement, the employer must have adequate insurance cover and the usual health and safety standards should be met. Until the law changes, asking companies to adhere to guidelines like these offers a more realistic method of protecting unpaid workers from extreme exploitation.'

For more information, visit **www.work-experience.org**.

Q: Employers seem more interested in work experience than my academics. Was my degree a waste of time?

A: They might not be jumping up and down about your academic achievements, but very few employers say a degree is useless. It's just that now that so many people have one, it's no longer seen as the icing on the cake, it's just the, er, cake. The point is that it's difficult for employers to distinguish between graduates and so the right work experience at least reassures them that you have developed some directly relevant skills, gained an insight into the sector and demonstrated commitment.

Q: I can't even get a work experience placement – because they say I don't have any experience! What can I do?

A: Ah yes, the work experience vicious circle. You need experience in order to get experience. Many grads find they face this frustrating – and seemingly unsolvable – conundrum. But there is a way around it. It involves lowering your standards – just temporarily. While I'm a big fan of aiming high (applying to all the best places first), if you find you aren't having any joy, you might need to move the bar a little lower, to help you get your foot in the door.

For example, if you're finding it difficult to get a break in investment banking, some experience in retail banking could make things easier. If you want to become a researcher, working as a lab technician for a while can boost your CV. If you aren't having any luck landing a placement at a major TV channel then try the smaller production companies instead. In any profession, once you've got some experience under your belt, you can re-apply for to your first-choice places. Your odds will be much better, now your CV looks that much stronger.

Q: How can I find out about work experience placements?

A: Informal placements in some sectors such as working in art galleries, music management, advertising are not always advertised. Nor are all placements at small or medium-sized companies – largely because these organisations don't always know that they need someone until you call! It's also worth knowing that unpaid placements are rarely advertised because employers can get into hot water for recruiting for a 'job' that undermines the minimum wage laws. For these reasons, finding out about opportunities often means ringing, e-mailing or writing to employers directly and asking them whether they run any sort of internships, work experience placements or can arrange work shadowing (and if so, how to apply for these opportunities – every company is different). This might feel like a shot in the dark, but they'll probably be used to approaches like this, and be impressed that you're demonstrating initiative.

In other sectors such as finance and law, internships are advertised quite widely, and well in advance (often for a June internship you'll need to apply the previous November). Ads for these will appear on their websites and through graduate career directories, university careers centres and on job boards.

The golden rules of work experience:

- ☑ **Do** take the work as seriously as a proper paid job. This is your chance to show what you'd be like to work with if they offered you a permanent job.
- ☒ **Don't** expect anyone to remember your name on day one. If placements last two weeks, the team will meet 26 people like you every year...
- ☒ **Don't** worry about 'standing out'. Have faith that if you're reliable, efficient and upbeat, they'll remember you.
- ☒ **Don't** assume the placement will turn into a job. It probably won't, so line up other options so you aren't disappointed. If they do offer you a job, you can always cancel any pre-arranged placements elsewhere. Most likely, there will be a queue of other people waiting to take your place.
- ☑ **Do** know your place. Bugging the boss and butting into conversations is not a good look.

- ☑ **Do** look out for opportunities to demonstrate initiative – people may not always have time to stop work and give you instructions. If you're twiddling your thumbs and see something that needs doing, ask your supervisor 'Would it be helpful if I...?'
- ☒ **Don't** be a maverick. There's a fine line between showing initiative and being a loose cannon. Always check before you take action.
- ☑ **Do** keep in touch when the placement comes to an end.
- ☑ **Do** keep an eye out for forthcoming vacancies.
- ☒ **Don't** bug the boss to give you a job.
- ☑ **Do** volunteer to do the rubbish jobs. You might feel like a loser making the tea, but it's a great way to get to know the team and it shows you're keen to make a good impression.
- ☑ **Do** tell them or e-mail them to say how much you've enjoyed the placement when it comes to an end. Choose the person you got on with the best, and ask them to let you know if any vacancies come up in the future.

66 It's all about attitude

The number one thing to remember is to be 'can-do' – at all times. Treat your placement like a real job – and it might just lead to one. From a week at one of the big TV companies, I was offered a weekend job as a runner and then a full-time position. No matter how menial the task I was given, I did it with a smile. Graduates worry about 'standing out' from the crowd but if you work hard, you will. Other 'workies' moaned about not being paid, and used it as an excuse to be sloppy and lazy but I just got on with doing my best. Who cares if they saw me as a suck-up? I landed a job – and they didn't. I now see work experience as a brilliant test for anyone who says they want to get into this industry. The people who really want it really try.

Jessica Gunn, 23

2:1, Contemporary Media Practice, University of Westminster

Further study

Do you miss having your nose in the books? Are you desperate to get back to the lab? Or do you just want to put off the real world for another year?

Think carefully. Postgraduate study can be hugely personally rewarding and a fantastic addition to your CV, whether you pursue an academic taught course (an MA, MSc or Postgraduate diploma), a research degree (a PhD) or a vocational course (such as journalism qualification the NTCJ). But remember that it's a big investment of both your time and money.

The upsides...

Postgraduate can help you develop extra maturity, self-reliance and independence. You're back at university, but this time you're starting your course older and wiser – and because you really want to be there. (As you know, many undergrads drift into their first degree – and it's hard not to be distracted by the social aspect of studying, at least in your first year.)

Getting back to the books or the lab can really boost your job prospects, too. It can:

- make you a more attractive candidate for the job market in certain sectors or for certain roles. In some cases it is either compulsory or at least expected to have a postgraduate qualification.
- help if you want to work overseas where higher qualifications are often more highly valued then in the UK.
- mean you start work on a higher salary.
- help you switch directions if you want to work in an area unrelated to your first degree. (For example, if an Economics graduate wants to move into international development, an MA in that subject can be very helpful. An Art History graduate

interested in arts marketing can benefit from an MSc in Marketing.)

- increase your credibility in a particular topic through gaining greater depth of knowledge.
- boost your confidence in your own abilities. When you believe you're a great candidate, it's far easier to sell yourself effectively in applications and interviews.

The downsides...

Unfortunately, whatever the prospectus says, there are no *guarantees* that further study will definitely make you a more attractive candidate for the job market – or start you on a higher salary. The literature for most courses will boast impressive success rates, but institutions have financial reasons for wanting you to sign up, so you can't always trust the marketing hype. It's best to check out the facts and seek impartial advice before you commit to anything.

Postgraduate study is seriously expensive – even if you get academic funding you'll probably need to pay for your own living expenses. It's also a big commitment – postgraduate courses can be up to two years long. In addition, there's also a small chance that if your course isn't relevant to your career – or you can't show how it enhances your worth to an employer – it could count against you later on, as employers might be given the impression you're indecisive or unable to commit.

 TOP TIP

If you decide to enrol in post grad study, it's worth shopping around. Don't be afraid to ask questions. *You're* the customer. If you can, visit the institutions and bring a list of questions to ask the staff, students and recent graduates.

There are so many courses – seek impartial advice

When I decided I wanted to do a PGCE and become a geography teacher, I didn't have a clue how to organise it. There were so many places I could study and I didn't know what to look for in a course. A friend told me we could still use our university careers centre even after we've graduated, so I drove to Cambridge and spent the day there. The resource library was brilliant and the staff really knew their stuff, and provided loads of info about the pros and cons of all the different colleges and courses. I've also done a bit of networking and spoken to two friends and five of my aunts who are all teachers, or training to be teachers. They've given me some great advice about which courses are supposed to be the best taught – and the most fun!

Megan Tierney, 21

2:1, Geography, University of Cambridge

Does postgraduate study impress employers?

Sometimes, but not always, says Alistair Leathwood, Managing Director of recruitment consultancy FreshMinds Talent...

'Most employers divide further study into two types: the seriously intellectual variety and the vocational "this-should-make-me-a-stronger-candidate" variety. From an employer's point of view, the jury is still out on how much (if anything) either actually adds. While a super-academic PhD is undoubtedly impressive, it's unlikely to be any more *valuable* in an employer's eyes than the same amount of time spent gaining work experience. And while practical vocational courses can be beneficial – or even necessary – in some industries (such as hotel management or news journalism), other employers aren't convinced about the value of extra qualifications, particularly in business-related subjects. As a general rule, I'd encourage people to do postgraduate study only if you really want to, because you really love the subject. If you know that isn't what's driving you, you're probably better off bagging some experience instead. Using postgraduate study as a stalling tactic and expecting it to pay off in the working world is a serious gamble.'

Further study – your questions answered

Q: How do I know if I really need to do another course?

A: Good question. It's wise to be aware that different sources will give you different advice – and for different reasons. Remember that universities need to make money, so it's in their interests to try and sell you a course. Just as you'd be suspicious of someone trying to sell you any type of product or service, it pays to take what they say with a pinch of salt. Don't be dazzled by statistics – these can easily be tweaked to sound as persuasive as possible.

The best way to find out whether you need another qualification is to ask people who are already in the job or industry that you think is right for you. What do they advise? Talk to more than one person – since typically people will advise you to do whatever they did.

Q: Is postgraduate study a good way to buy time if I don't know what I want to do? At least I'll have another qualification.

A: It's tempting to use postgraduate study as a stalling tactic, but remember that it's a seriously expensive one. Be honest – are you the kind of person who might never feel ready to take the plunge and start a proper job? If you suspect your main motivation for doing further study is putting off decision making, then remember that your initial job isn't as binding as you think it is. You don't have to stick with one career for life. (For more on this, see Chapter 2.) Once you've taken the pressure off yourself to find and start your 'dream career' right now, your next move should seem more manageable.

If the idea of taking a permanent job still brings you out in hives, remember that further study isn't your only option if you want to stay a free agent while you work out what's what. For example, it's worth investigating internships, which can offer a low-risk, low-commitment introduction to a workplace. Depending on the sector and role, the experience you gain might even be considered more valuable by employers than further study.

Q: Can't I just do postgraduate study for the sheer joy of it?

A: Of course you can. Many people do continue their studies because they love their subject and haven't had enough of it yet. But have your eyes wide open. If you decide to pursue this option, make sure you engage with thinking about life beyond the course whilst you're enjoying your academic studies. Remember, your extra qualification doesn't come with any guarantees of a better job or higher salary at the end. If money is an issue, check out all the funding options available. It might be better to just continue your passion as an interest outside work or consider returning to the subject later in life.

Q: Will a brilliant Masters degree disguise my dodgy Bachelors?

A: Occasionally, yes. A below-par Bachelor's degree can be offset with an impressive Masters – but not always. It really depends on the industry and the employer – so seek advice from prospective recruiters before you make the leap. Don't be surprised if some employers seem suspicious.

Furthermore, it's worth asking whether you're the right kind of person to take on the responsibility of a postgraduate course. It's a big commitment, so be honest with yourself. Are you considering further study because you really want to do it? Or because you're annoyed with yourself for not working harder for your Bachelors and embarrassed that you got a poor grade? If so, who's to say that your Masters *will* be impressive? Is it possible that you're just not cut out for academia? That you like the idea of it more than you enjoy putting the time in? Then I'd advise you to take the best job offer you can get and throw yourself into the working world. And who knows? You might well find that you're actually better at the practical side of life after all.

" My Masters made up for my disappointing Bachelors

I was gutted to only get a 2:2 for my Bachelors in Maths – and I knew that it would make it that much harder to land a job in investment management, which is what I wanted to do. Most financial services employers insist on at least a 2:1. In the absence of any job offers, I applied for work experience with a hedge fund company, as an introduction to the industry. I found I loved the work and wanted to learn more about it, so I started considering a Masters. I didn't want to waste my time or money, so asked my dad's friend (who's in investment management) for advice. We concluded that in my case, further education would boost my employability. During my Masters, I made some great contacts, including a head-hunter who put me in touch with the company I now work for. Postgrad study isn't right for everyone, but for me it was the best thing I could have done.

Robert Hall, 24
2:2, Maths, Bristol University
MA Investment Management, Cass Business School,
City of London University "

Q: How do I know if a course is right for me?

A: First, ask yourself what you are aiming to get out of your studies and exactly how this will help you achieve your longer term goals (finding a job in the field you're interested in). Will employers only consider you once you've obtained the specialist knowledge that can only be gained through this course? Will having this extra qualification boost your credibility? (Are you sure? Seek impartial advice.) Will your studies increase your exposure to potential employers (i.e. Will it mean working with companies who might be able to offer you a job later)? Which course will give you the best possible chance of gaining the most?

Next, think about which employers will want to buy this experience from you when you've finished. Are you sure employers you want to work with rate this course as highly as you think? Do they teach on it? Can you use your course to make contact with them – or even do a project for them?

Q: I've decided to go for it – how can I make the most of my postgraduate study?

A: By all means throw yourself into your studies – after all, that's what you're there for – but don't switch off your career radar altogether. University can feel like a closed system, but keep thinking *beyond* the course, and use your spare time wisely to research your career options thoroughly. If you didn't make good use of your careers service as an undergraduate, now is the time. Check out what they offer in terms of events, talks, courses, training. To boost your exposure to possible employers, consider choosing a subject or dissertation which will enable you to approach relevant employers and even do something that is useful for them. It's not uncommon for post grads to land jobs off the back of a Masters project done in conjunction with an employer. And finally, make as many useful contacts as you can. Take the time to talk to lecturers (both permanent and visiting), who may have the inside track on interesting new jobs related to your field of study.

Postgraduate study: the checklist

Shopping around? It pays to know what you're looking for, say The Careers Group...

For all postgraduate study, ask them:
What are the entry requirements and will I meet them?
When do I need to apply?
How much are the fees and likely living costs?
Is funding available? How do I apply? What are my chances?
Where have previous graduates found employment?

And ask yourself...
If I don't get funding, how will I pay for it?
What do I plan to do afterwards?

For research degrees, ask them:

What percentage of past students finished their research successfully?

How good are the research facilities?

Who will be my supervisor? What's their background and can I meet them?

And ask yourself...

In what area do I want to do research?

Is my prospective supervisor academically suitable, approachable and likely to be available throughout my research degree? Can I get on with them?

For academic taught courses, ask them:

What are the compulsory elements in the course – and what is optional?

What are the teaching methods?

Who are the tutors and how often will I see them?

Is there a project or dissertation and what does it involve?

Does this course include opportunities to do placements or meet employers?

For vocational courses, ask:

How many previous students found employment related to the course?

What help do the tutors give in finding suitable work afterwards?

Does this course include opportunities to do placements or meet employers?

Travelling

Considering escaping to travel the world? Clearly there are lots of good reasons to go – and yes, now is an obvious time to head for the hills (or sand dunes).

But think about your reasons first... What's motivating you? Genuine wanderlust – or a fear of facing up to reality?

The upsides...

With no job to resign from and no flat to sub-let, many graduates say the end of university is the perfect time to go travelling. After the stress of finals, a change of scene might be exactly what you need before getting stuck into finding a first job that will give you some great experience and be a stepping-stone to other roles further down the line. After the rigid structure of tutorials and exams, getting away from it all can be a fantastic way to clear some head-space.

Spending time abroad can also be a welcome addition to your CV. For example, it can:

- demonstrate to employers that you're mature and self-sufficient, with a broad outlook on the world (especially if you decide to work abroad for at least part of your trip)
- develop transferable skills (like communication and organisation) that will improve your employability once you get home
- give you some good material for interviews

The downsides...

If you don't know what you want to do job-wise when you go away, you're unlikely to be any the wiser once you get back. Graduates often hope that 'clearing their head' is all it takes for their 'dream career' to magically occur to them, so that when they get home, they can just get on with it. This almost never happens (more of which below).

Travelling is very expensive, so it's also worth knowing that there are no guarantees that travelling will make you any more employable when you get home. Although some employers value travel in its own right, as a general rule, time abroad will only make you more employable if you work while you're out there. Lying on a beach in Brazil or partying in Goa doesn't show you've learnt anything useful. Just having a great tan doesn't make you more attractive to employers.

If you have a great time, getting back can be a major comedown. Grads who have been away for a long period often experience 'reverse culture shock', which can be unsettling. Getting back into the swing of day-to-day reality can take time.

How do employers view time spent travelling?

A waste of time and money – or valuable life experience? Alistair Leathwood, Managing Director of recruitment consultancy FreshMinds Talent explains...

'Graduates often agonise over whether to go travelling – but the truth is that very few employers care either way. Some companies want people who are obsessive about work and can't wait to get cracking – but most prefer their employees to be a bit more balanced. Although in most cases travel doesn't add as much to your CV as work experience, it can definitely benefit your application. For a start, it suggests you have a broader outlook than someone who has come straight from uni and it proves you can exist outside an educational institution, which is also reassuring for employers. If you have any kind of job while you're away, that's even better. To graduates who worry about being behind their friends career-wise when they return, I say that's really up to you. You're the only person who will mind – and in five years' time, it won't make a blind bit of difference that you took a year out. If you want to go travelling now, then go!'

66 Mexico opened my eyes

I didn't have a clue about the direction of my career after graduation so I packed my bags for a year and went off to Mexico get some life experience. But I didn't want to spend a year lazing on beaches. I enrolled on a one-month intensive CELTA course (teaching English in a foreign language) before I left. Once in Mexico, I quickly landed a job teaching English to staff in smart hotels. I had a fantastic time – my confidence soared. I was aware of the useful experience I was gaining every day I was away, from leadership and teaching to dealing with people from all walks of life. I'm considering trying for jobs in the media industry, but if that doesn't work out or I need to earn money in other ways first, then I'll always have the teaching qualification and experience as a Plan B. Coming back was a bit of a shock, but I feel wiser – like I've grown up a lot – and now see the world from a different perspective.

Amy McCallum, 22

2:1, Drama and Theatre Arts, University of Birmingham

66 I realised I'd just be running away

I was so tempted to go travelling when I graduated – but I'm so glad now that I didn't. For me, it would just have been an excuse to delay making decisions about jobs. Instead, I've spent the time applying for jobs, going for interviews and temping. It sounds boring compared to globe-trotting, but the practical office experience has been brilliant – especially since I haven't made up my mind exactly what I want to do as a proper 'first job'. I can't wait to see more of the world when I feel a bit more secure. To really enjoy the experience, you've got to go for the right reasons, when you're in the right frame of mind, not just because you want to run away from reality.

Julia Edwards, 22

2:1, European Studies, Durham University

66 I went travelling – to Brighton!

My head was spinning when I left university – I just wanted to relax and take some time out to get myself together. Some of my friends went to Africa or Asia, but I decided to stay closer to home and moved to Brighton for a year! In many ways it was like a gap year. OK, I wasn't building huts or climbing mountains but I'd still escaped from *my* reality. I decided to put off the heavy question of what my career was going to be – at least for a while. Instead, I applied for roles working for local government and charities, and landed a job doing youth work. It was amazing – I had so much fun. And it totally changed my perspective once I came back to London.

Demelza Bowyer, 25

2:1, Modern and Medieval Language, University of Cambridge 99

Travelling – your questions answered

Q: I'm desperate to go travelling but don't want to get left behind job-wise. Should I go – or stay and get cracking with my career?

A: If there's a particular country you've always wanted to visit, or an appealing project has presented itself to you, there's nothing to stop you from grabbing it with both hands. The main thing is that your time away should feel like a positive step – like you're *gaining* something, not just avoiding something. As long as you have realistic expectations about what time abroad will and probably won't change, there's no reason why you shouldn't seize the opportunity. The job market will still be here when you get back. On the other hand, the country you want to visit will still be there for you to visit at a later date, if you do decide to work for a while first. It's really up to you.

Q: If I don't go now – I'll never go. But is that a good enough reason to go travelling?

A: It's entirely up to you. But who says you'll never go if you don't go now? Remember, careers and employers are much more flexible than they were, and many workers take sabbatical years out of their jobs, or go off to help charities such as Voluntary Service Overseas (VSO), where the average age for volunteers is 38, and most placements last two years. Organisations like VSO only place people who have already developed professional skills. If you really want to help, you might actually be more useful in a few years' time.

It's also worth remembering that many companies have offices internationally, and might be open to sending you to New York, Hong Kong or Sydney once you've bagged some experience here in the UK. Working abroad needn't mean digging wells – it could simply mean doing your existing job in another country.

Q: I don't know what I want to do job-wise. Might inspiration strike while I'm away?

A: It's possible – but don't bank on it. Lots of graduates jet off in the hope that their true dream will occur to them once they've had a chance to get away and clear their head. The idea that you might 'find yourself' during your time away is seductive – but probably not realistic. What you'll actually do is become absorbed in the moment and forget about reality altogether.

As for having time to job-hunt while you're away, this will depend on your travel plans. If you take a temp job in an office in Sydney, you might have a chance to do some research. But if you're hiking in Nepal and come across an Internet cafe, are you really going to surf for jobs? Or are you more likely to e-mail your mum?

Inspiration is particularly unlikely to strike if you don't do any proper work while you're away. You might find out more about yourself personally, but if you aren't testing yourself in a proper workplace you'll be no closer to discovering what you enjoy and don't enjoy in a job. This needn't be a disaster, of course. It's just a good idea to be realistic when you go, so you won't hit a major slump when you get back.

Q: I've decided to go – but I'm only going to do fun, low-paid casual work while I'm out there. When I get back, will employers mind?

A: It all depends on which employers you intend to target when you get back. More 'serious' work might look better on your CV – but bar work and au pairing aren't a total disaster. It's a question of making the most of whatever experience you do have by highlighting the transferable skills you've picked up, such as organisation and communication.

Q: How can I make the most of my time abroad?

A: If you don't know what you want to do when you get back...

- Have an outcome in mind. What do you want to achieve from your trip that will be beneficial when it comes to applying for jobs? For example, do you want to experience a different culture? Learn a new language? Make a difference to the world? Knowing why you're going will make it more likely that you get something out of your trip that you can sell to employers when you get back.
- Maximise your exposure. Experiment with a wide variety of activities so that you can test out your likes and dislikes and find out more about yourself and your strengths and weaknesses. If you get the chance to work, take note of what you enjoy and what you don't.
- Talk to everybody while you're away. Take an interest in what they do and have done and why. This can be a fantastic way of expanding the breadth and depth of your knowledge about careers options.

If you do know what you want to do when you get back...

- Tie up loose ends before you go. Do plenty of research before you leave so that you are aware of any deadlines that might happen while you are away.
- Recruit 'eyes and ears' to spot job opportunities for you while you're away, and forward them on to you by e-mail. Depending on the nature of your travel plans, you might even be able to apply for jobs while you're away, so you can line up a couple of meetings or interviews for when you get back.
- Try to bag some relevant experience while you're out there. It will come in handy for interviews when you get back.

In Chapter 9...
How to take charge of your day-to-day job-hunt.

NOTES

Part 4:
Tips and
tricks

**Lots of little
ways to make
your life easier**

NOTES

Chapter 9:
Healthy habits

Ideas to kick-start your job-hunt, get organised, chart your progress and stay motivated...

Things are looking up! Knowing what you're looking for and how to start hunting is half the battle.

That said, it pays to be prepared for the rest of the task ahead. Whether you're dead keen to get cracking with your job-hunt or dreading it more than your own funeral, actually knuckling down and getting on with it can be harder than you think.

Of course, how easy or hard you find it depends on all sorts of random variables. How self-disciplined are you? How motivated do you feel? What sector have you chosen? How realistic are your expectations? And how much time do you have to dedicate to your job-hunt? (Although, weirdly, grads with less time often find they're actually *more* efficient.)

Whatever your circumstances, it definitely pays to have a few tricks up your sleeve.

The following gems come from graduates who have gone before you – and learnt the hard way. You'll see that they're all pro-active methods for staying in control of your time – and your mind.

'Yikes! – *my mind*?' Yes, I'm afraid so. You'll discover that the job-hunt isn't just about job ads, CVs and interviews. A huge slice of the pie is down to psychological resilience. It's a mind-game. It's about remembering *why* you're putting yourself through all this. It's about being kind to yourself – but not so kind you don't actually do anything. Putting safety nets in place for when things go wrong. And finding little ways to help you work better, so that you *feel* better.

Healthy habit: the motivation checklist

What: Your tailor-made list of the five strongest forces driving you to find your great first job. And – if you need some extra 'fire' under you – the five serious downers that will happen if you *don't* get your act together.

When: Ideally, do this before you start your job-hunt. The sooner the better – but it's never too late. You'll find the motivation checklist useful whenever you do it.

Genius because... Articulating what's driving you – yes, you're going to actually write it down – will help you focus on the task ahead. Plus, your list will make an invaluable reference tool for moments when the going gets tough.

How to do it: Easy-peasy. Just complete the two lists below.

'I want to get a great first job so that...'

List any reasons you like and be as honest as possible. What are your core motivators? Getting out of your crappy temping job? Working with people you actually like? Finding work that makes you think? Showing the world you're not the useless loser they think you are? Making your parents proud? Money? Status? Glory?

1. ....

2. ....

3. ....

4. ....

5. ....

'If I don't find a great first job, I can see myself...'

What will happen if you *don't* get your act together and go for it? Visualise what will happen if you do nothing about your job-hunt – in other words, if you just coast along, doing whatever you're doing now. What would happen? Might you end up living with your parents forever? Would you be too poor to afford to go out with your friends, or save enough to go travelling? Would you hate going to work every morning? Would you feel like a failure? Go on – really *go there*. Scare yourself!

1. ....

2. ....

3. ....

4. ....

5. ....

Healthy habit: the five-minute day plan

What: Today's 'to-do' list. You set the target, you achieve the target. Hardly a revolutionary idea, I know. But if you use your five minutes planning time wisely you'll be amazed by the difference it makes. Not only will your output rocket, but it will also help you feel good about yourself and your achievements.

When: At the beginning of any day you're going to spend working on your job-hunt. You can also do it for your week ahead if you're working full-time and squeezing in job-hunting tasks when you can, or just for an evening, if that's all the time you have.

Genius because... It pays to plan how you're going to use your time before you actually start. It helps you see each dawn as a new day. Yesterday wasn't so good? Today will be better. It also gives you a practical list of do-able tasks to focus on. Everybody needs little targets to meet, or we'd never do anything. Plus, it gives you sense of achievement. By crossing off all your items at the end of the day, you'll feel proud of yourself, and able to go to the pub feeling you've had a good day, rather than an OK or bad day. You might even have picked up some momentum – meaning tomorrow should be easier still.

How to do it: follow these instructions...

1. Write the day at the top of a blank page.
2. Take five minutes to make a list of 5–10 mini-tasks you would definitely like to get done today. Make your tasks bite-sized and realistic. They should be small and self-contained enough to be do-able, e.g. 'Finish application form for [job a]', 'Make appointment with [recruitment agency] for next week' or 'Go through job ads from the weekend newspapers', but not *Find dream job*.
3. Ask yourself: 'Have I given myself enough to do? Or too much?' Be realistic, so that you can look at the list and think, 'Yes, if I get all these things done by the end of the day, I'll be happy.'
4. Resolve not to get side-tracked.
5. Get started and cross off each task as you go.

TOP TIP

Write your five-minute day plan before you switch on your computer in the morning. It's all too easy to get distracted by e-mail or the Internet and never get around to it.

Healthy habit: the hour-by-hour schedule

What: A guideline of how you're going to spend your day – created by you. You'll find an hour-by-hour schedule especially useful when you've blocked out a large stretch of time to spend on your job-hunt. It works on the same principles as a revision planner.

When: Before you start a full day of job-hunting.

Genius because... It helps you take control – and stay in control – of your time. The tasks on your hour-by-hour chart are short and self-contained.

Having an outline of your day will help you stay focussed on getting the smaller tasks done, one by one, so you don't feel totally overwhelmed and instead do nothing at all.

How to do it: Quickly. If revision planners never worked for you, was one of the reasons that you spent *way* too long making yours look pretty? And nowhere near long enough time actually doing the work you had scheduled in? Me too! Drawing up your hour-by-hour schedule should take five minutes, tops. It's a basic tool that no one but you is ever going to see. So lose the highlighter pens. And don't even think about laminating it.

The hour-by-hour planner

Your hour-by-hour planner should look like this:

10.00 – go through job ads from weekend newspapers
11.00 – research [job a]
11.30 – 10 minute tea break – check/write personal e-mails
12.00 – e-mail Mum's friend about meeting up
13.00 – LUNCH HOUR – eat healthy sandwich/salad and get some fresh air.
14.00 – background research into [new sector I've heard about]
15.00 – phone recruitment agency to chase for vacancies
15.30 – 10 minute tea break – check/write personal e-mails
16.00 – find names of five other recruitment agencies who work in my sector
17.00 – e-mail Uncle Pete's friend to thank him for meeting up yesterday

 TOP TIP

Think about when you're at your most productive. Make sure you do your most challenging jobs at the time of day when you're on top form.

Healthy habit: the progress chart

What: A central place to keep track of your 'spinning plates' – or live job applications. Your progress chart should include the date you applied, your contact's details and what action is due to happen next (for example, when do you plan to chase progress, if you don't hear anything from the employer?). It can take any form you like. It could be a Word document, an Excel spreadsheet – or a low-tech pen and ink wall-chart. Whatever works for you.

When: As soon as possible – although you might want to wait to start your progress chart when you have a few achievements to write on it.

Genius because... It's a visual representation of your job-hunt. Seeing how much you've done will give you confidence, and seeing what you still have to do will help you focus. Having these tasks swirling around in your head can't compete with seeing them in black and white.

How to do it: Design it however you like – just make sure it works for you. The most important thing is that it's quick and easy to update. Progress charts work best when you think of them as living, breathing documents – so get into the habit of updating it whenever you achieve something, or think of a new task that needs to be done. (This shouldn't be hard to remember – it's nice to see when you're making progress.) Make your progress chart your new best friend. If you find you're not using it, that's probably because it's in the wrong format for you. Try every way you can – and stick with your favourite.

TOP TIP

Remember, you should always have at least five live applications on the go. And don't get fixated on one job over the others. (Yes, even if you really, really *really* want it...)

Why is it important to get into good habits?

Gael Lindenfield, psychotherapist and author of *Finding your Get Up and Go,* explains why it pays to be proactive…

'As graduates quickly discover, job-hunting is – and feels – completely different from being at university. There's no imposed structure and you don't have your friends there for support. If you're back living at home, things can be even tougher.

'If you struggled with motivation and self-discipline as a student, don't be surprised if you find you're struggling again now. Learning to focus and discipline yourself is a skill that takes years to hone – just ask anyone who runs their own business, or works from home. People say 'Treat your job-hunt like a job' – but for most graduates it just isn't realistic to expect them to be that productive. And setting the bar that high will only set them up to fall far below it.

'Instead, graduates should take a pro-active approach, making simple changes to their routine in order to increase their productivity. (Trust me, this is a much better idea than hoping to become super-efficient and motivated overnight – when you never have been before.) The most important thing is not to lose touch with the outside world. If you're at home alone all day, you'll quickly start to feel isolated and your confidence will drop. If you're job-hunting from home, get out of the house for at least a few hours, even if it's to do non-job-hunt related errands. When you get back, you'll be far more productive.

'Job-hunters should also keep an eye on what works for them – and what doesn't. Keep tweaking your routine so that you get the most out of your day as you can. Forget about being 100 per cent efficient. Instead, be

Healthy habit: refine your routine

What: Your individual quest to discover how to get the most out of the time you spend job-hunting. Make it your business to stay hyper-aware of what works for you and what doesn't. If you're job-hunting full-time or at the weekends, you might find you work better in the mornings if you start your day by going out to buy a newspaper and a cappuccino or that a run round the block is a brilliant way to get you out of your afternoon slump. If you're job-hunting mid-week around other work, you might find you achieve more in your lunch breaks at the local internet cafe than sitting at your desk at the office.

When: All the time – good days *and* bad days. Keep assessing how well your routine is working, and try new ideas to shake things up. Don't be surprised if what works for you keeps changing. If your output suddenly drops off, this is probably just a sign it's time to try something new instead. Stay aware of your productivity and be prepared to tweak your routine if it isn't working as well as it once did.

Genius because... Hand-crafting your routine takes into account that we're all different – and what works for one person won't work for another. (Plus, we all play different mind-games with ourselves!) This way, you can tailor-make your own routine, so that you get the most out of each day. It's also one of the few ways you can turn an unproductive day into something useful another day. So there's no such thing as a wasted day.

How to do it: The key is to be super-conscious of what's working for you, and what isn't. If you have a good day, ask yourself why it went so well – did you do anything differently? If so, then do that again tomorrow. Likewise, if you have a bad day, try to pinpoint why it never quite took off. Do things differently tomorrow.

Are you a lark or an owl?

The experts now believe there are physiological reasons why some of us are morning people while others are night owls. If you're a 'lark' whose energy and alertness dip in the afternoon, that's the best time to take a stroll. This should wake your body up. If you're an 'owl' and struggle in the mornings, try leaving your curtains open at night so you wake up gently when the sun comes up. Get outside as early in the day as possible so your body gets its fix of mood-boosting natural light. If you can't go outside, have your cuppa by the sunniest window in your house or flat.

From *The Body Clock Guide to Better Health*, Michael Smolensky and Lynne Lamberg.

Healthy habit: the parental summit

What: You and the folks in a sit-down situation, talking about your job-hunt. If you're living back at home, the parental summit is particularly useful. Having you back under their roof when you're all used to having more space is stressful enough, without them feeling like they're treading on eggshells over the highly flammable issue of, 'What you're going to do, darling, you know, *next*..?' Even if you've moved out, the parental summit is a good idea, to help you handle their phone calls.

When: As soon as you feel confident that you have a decent job-hunt plan of action.

Genius because... It's a pre-emptive strike. Keeping your parents in the loop is a good idea all round – it stops them hovering nervously (or bugging you blatantly), and makes you face your fear of them asking what you're up to. By coming to *them*, you're putting yourself in control of the situation. Plus, they might even be able to help. If not with actual advice or contacts, then with support in whatever form you find most useful.

How to do it: 'The goal is to reach an understanding that respects everybody's needs', explains Gael Lindenfield, psychotherapist and author of *Assert Yourself*. 'During the meeting, remember to listen to each other. All families are different and some parents will find this time harder than others – in different ways and for different reasons.' What next? Gael suggests the following:

1. Thank them. 'Show you appreciate all their support so far.'
2. Reassure them. 'Tell them that you have been a bit caught out by the reality of finishing uni, but you want things to improve now. If you like, show them your job-hunt action plan. It's up to you to decide how close you want them to be to your job-hunt – find an optimal distance that works for everybody.'
3. Let them help. 'If you like, and they want to feel useful, give them jobs to do, like cutting out job ads they see, or passing your CV to friends or colleagues.'
4. Return the favour. 'If you're living at home, offer to do household chores or run errands for them, so you feel you're contributing something. Far from being their skivvy, this will actually lift your self-esteem.'
5. Promise to be honest with each other. 'Don't be tempted to keep bad news from them. They'll prefer to know the truth – and anyway they'll be able to see when you're upset.'
6. Monitor the situation. 'Keep an eye on how your strategy is working. Then do more of what's working and less of what isn't.'

Healthy habit: the switch-off

What: The moment when you pack up your job-hunt kit and finish working on your job-hunt for the day.

When: This isn't school – 'going-home time' really is up to you. If you're job-hunting full-time or dedicating whole days to it at weekends, most people find their attention starts to drift by 5 or 6 p.m. If you've had a good day, that's a perfectly respectable time to stop. (On the

Parents are people too

Are they hovering around you – or trying desperately to play it cool? Just remember, they're struggling too, says Gael Lindenfield, psychotherapist and author of *Emotional Confidence*.

'It's easy for graduates to complain that their parents are pushy, nosy, patronising, snappy or just plain irritating. But just as this is a difficult time for you, remember that it's not much fun for them, either. Graduates grumble about being back at home – but what about their mum and dad? Don't forget, they've had the place to themselves while you were at university. Is it possible you're cramping their style as much as they're cramping yours?

'The busier you all are with your own lives, the better. But if you're all back under one roof, it's still easy to slip back into your old 'Parent v Child' mode, where your mum does the cooking and you spend lots of time in your room and throw the odd tantrum at the dinner table. Resist. I know you're feeling vulnerable, but it's important for all of you that you behave like an adult – looking like a lost toddler or a stroppy teenager is likely to trigger a strong reaction in your parents. So watch what you say, how you dress and your body language too. Try not to look sad all the time, don't slouch, and make an effort with your appearance. You'll feel better, and your parents won't treat you like a child.'

other hand, if you didn't get going until 4 p.m., you might want to crack on a bit longer, to try and salvage something from the day.) If you're squeezing some mid-week job-hunting around full-time work, you'll still need to 'switch off' before bed or your mind could race all night.

Genius because... If you don't have a clear end to your day, you probably don't have a clear start either. Marking the difference between working and time off is crucial. This isn't like studying at uni, when you just did it whenever you had time. The job-hunt should be more structured. Clocking on and clocking off should mark a change in your mindset.

How to do it: Don't just shut down your computer and leg it to the pub. Instead, take a moment to go back to your five-minute day plan and assess how many tasks you managed to achieve today. If you've completed all (or most) of them, congratulate yourself. If you've hardly done anything, take a moment to feel cross with yourself and promise to have a better day tomorrow. Remember to assess your routine, too. How much did you achieve today? Was there any particular reason why today was a great (or terrible) day? If it was a real corker of a day, ask yourself why. Is this a winning recipe for success you can repeat tomorrow? Then jot down any tasks you must do tomorrow, and vow to focus on getting all of them completed to make up for your bad day today. *Then* go to the pub.

Healthy habit: the friend plan

What: Your strategy for dealing with your peers.

When: As soon as possible.

Genius because... You'll be seeing a lot of them – and they're the closest people to understanding that situation you're in, so they potentially have a lot of influence on how you feel about yourself. If they're helpful, harnessing their emotional support can boost your morale and their practical support can be a great asset too (try meeting for coffee and then going to your local library or Internet cafe together). If your friends aren't helpful to be around, you need to know how to screen them out.

How to do it: You can't stop yourself comparing your own life with those of your friends, so don't even try, says Gael Lindenfield, psychotherapist and author of *The Self Esteem Bible*. 'The best thing to do is take some control of how you let your friends influence you. Choose who you compare yourself with – make sure they're people who have a positive influence on you, rather than a negative one.' Here, Gael shares more of her wisdom:

1. Hang out with good influences. 'Look for people who share your values and aspirations. Avoid friends who are too jokey, too self-centred or too stressed to care genuinely about you.'

2. Don't dodge successful friends. 'Yes, it can be galling to hear how well they're doing when you're finding things tough. But envy can be motivating, too.'

3. Discuss disappointment properly. 'If you're turned down for a job, by all means phone a friend who will cheer you up – but make sure you talk through your upset first. It's tempting to brush away feelings by saying, "I didn't want the stupid job anyway," but if that isn't true it can actually have a negative impact. Burying your disappointment without acknowledging it will only let it build. Accepting and acknowledging it will let you move on in a much healthier way.'

In Chapter 10...
How to get back on top if you hit rock bottom.

Chapter 10:
Rescue remedies

Is your output dipping towards zero? Has your get-up-and-go gone? Discover how to save yourself from disaster.

How are you getting on?

Some of you will have taken to the job-hunt like little fluffy ducks to water – feeling confident and motivated, and busy ticking things off your to-do list, applying for vacancies and going to interviews. If this is you, big congrats – you won't be needing this chapter.

But I suspect that not all of you will be doing so well with the task ahead – for all sorts of reasons…

- If you're working full-time, are you struggling to find the time around your day job?
- If you're at home all day, are you having trouble getting up and getting going?
- When you do find the time to invest in your job-hunt, do you find it hard to stay focussed on the task in hand?
- Do you feel busy – but also like you're not really getting anywhere?
- Are you feeling the squeeze from friends and family who keep asking perkily, 'How's the job-hunt going?'

Don't panic – you're not beyond help. You probably don't have serious psychological issues. And it's unlikely that you're just bone idle. Most likely, there's something else stopping you. The good news is that whatever it is that's paralysing you, it can be fixed. This chapter will show you how.

As I mentioned in Chapter 9, a huge portion of the job-hunt has nothing to do with CVs and interviews – it's about *you*. Your level of motivation, confidence and self-esteem is a crucial part of the job-hunt equation.

Weirdly, it's the one thing that's almost always forgotten by everyone who is trying to help you! Parents, friends, careers books and most careers counsellors don't appreciate the enormous impact that the way a job-hunting graduate *feels* will have on your level of output. As much as they want to help you, they're just not in the same psychological space as you are right now. People who are feeling motivated and confident can't understand why you can't just get on with it.

The only people who understand are those who have stood in your shoes – and can remember what it really feels like to be in your situation.

If you've read Chapter 1, you'll know you're not alone. Thousands of graduates are in the same boat as you. And *I* know how it feels, because I've been there too. I know it's rubbish. I know you *feel* rubbish. And I understand that it's not always as simple as just getting on with it.

So why is getting motivated for the job-hunt so difficult?

It's a complicated task

Firstly, it's a more complex task than people imagine. 'Go and find a job' sounds like a time-consuming, but ultimately *straightforward* mission. It isn't. It's made up of lots of little tasks – and each one requires motivation and determination to get it done.

In some ways, trying to get a job is like planning a trip to the cinema. Just as you can't simply 'go and get a job', you can't just 'go and see a film'. First, you need to choose a film you want to see, which means finding out what's on, and what's recommended, either by friends or by critics. Then, you need to find out which cinemas near your home or your work are showing that film. Then you need to find a friend who also wants to see that film. Then you need to find out when they're free. Then you need to make sure the film showing at a time you can both make. Then you need to book the ticket. Then you need to arrange a time to meet before the film. And then you need to find the motivation to actually get there. Even if it's dark and raining. Actually getting your bum on the seat of the movie theatre takes an awful lot of work. Likewise, there are multiple steps involved in finding a job – and each one requires you to be focussed, determined and motivated to actually do it.

There's no end in sight

Another tricky thing about job-hunting is that you can't pace yourself – because you don't know when your task is going to be finished. You might land the first job you apply for – but more than likely it will take a fair bit more work than that. But how much? *When* will you land your first job? Of course, no one can tell you that.

We're used to being able to see a 'light at the end of the tunnel' – but with the job-hunt you don't have that. Your task is over when you receive a job offer from a company you like, for a job you want. The light only appears when you reach the very end of the tunnel. But up until that moment, you have no idea whether it will be days, weeks or even months before you get your job.

Even worse, it's easy to become excited about getting to the final stages of the selection process for a job you really want – and mistake 'things looking positive' for being that light you're straining so hard to see. But they're very different things – and when that rejection letter comes in the post, you realise it. If that job was the only thing keeping you going, the days that follow can be very dark indeed.

There are psychological obstacles to hurdle

A common belief is that job-hunting is exhausting because it's a constant battle with employers. But for bright young graduates like you, this might not be the case. You might find that the hardest part isn't finding jobs to apply for, or getting your CV perfect. You can do that with your eyes closed. No, it's the battle with *yourself* that's the real nightmare.

You've probably already discovered that you are not a machine. As much as you might want to you can't 'just get on with it'. Because tangled up with the need to perform various administrative tasks (working on your CV, filling in applications, preparing for interviews) is a whole range of doubts and fears, generated by your own anxious little mind.

Fear of failure, loss of confidence, frustration at your low productivity... The impact of that appalling ratio of good days (when you achieve lots) to bad days (when you achieve little – or nothing at all). Grand Canyon-sized dips in your motivation and confidence, when it can seem impossible to ever climb out... Is any of this sounding familiar?

The good news is that when the enemy is *yourself*, at least you know it's a battle you can win. However deep a slump you find yourself in, there is always a way out. (I should know – I've had some real shockers.) And your chances are even better now that I'm supplying you with the tools. Remember Batman's utility belt? Well, think of this chapter as yours. I've loaded it with secret weapons for you to use when you find yourself in a tight spot. You'll see that I've covered the main difficulties faced by graduates struggling with the job-hunting process. For each, I've come up with solutions for you to try.

But – there's a 'but'. Although I'm providing you with the tools, it's *you* who's going to have to use them. Make no mistake – I may have called this chapter 'Rescue Remedies', but I'm not going to rescue you. You're going to do that yourself. Never forget that this job-hunt is *your* responsibility. It's up to *you* to get your act together.

What if you can't muster the energy? You will. When you get to the point when you want it badly enough and when you're so annoyed with yourself for *not* doing it, you'll do it.

Why is it so easy to stall?

Lost your mojo? Why psychotherapist and author of *Believing You Can Do It* Gael Lindenfield isn't surprised…

'The hardest part about job-hunting has nothing to do with the tedious task of sending off CVs. What causes graduates to lose momentum is the fact that it's so *emotionally* draining. Many graduates kick off their job-hunt without really understanding how difficult it's going to be, or suspecting it might be tough but feeling determined to "think positive".

'If you've lost motivation, it's probably because just "thinking positive" wasn't the right strategy for you – and as a result you haven't paced yourself properly for what could be a fairly long and arduous journey. Yes, you need a positive frame of mind, but it's important to be realistic too. Never kid yourself that the task ahead is easy, or tell yourself you're "nearly there". It will probably be a long, difficult journey. If it isn't, then that's a bonus.

'Expect to have both good days and bad days. On bad days, it can help to repeat mantras like "It may be hard but it's not impossible". You might also find it helpful to use psychological support strategies to help you manage stress and bounce back from setbacks, such as confidence and positive thinking boosters, relaxation exercises and self-esteem building activities. What then? Pick an action plan and get on with it.'

The problem: 'I can't find the time'

If you're working full-time, it can be a struggle to squeeze the job-hunt around your busy days. You're knackered in the evenings – and you want to spend your weekends having fun with your friends, not looking for jobs.

Unfortunately, I can't help you magic extra time out of thin air. You're going to have to find it within your existing routine. So take a good look at how you spend your time and see where you can wedge some job-hunting in. The chances that you are already a 100 per cent efficient machine are somewhat slim. There will be 'windows' you aren't currently using. And if you can't find any, look harder. They're there.

The rescue remedies:

Take time off

If you're temping, put a week aside and tell your agency you can't work that week. If you can't afford to take a whole week off, ask whether you can have the odd day here and there. Sometimes temp positions are more flexible than you think. If you can't wangle time off, try the following remedies...

Get yourself organised

If discipline doesn't come naturally, you're going to have to try harder, or this job thing isn't going to happen. Every week, make a list of tasks you want to get done (look back to the five-minute day plan, but make yours weekly, rather than daily).

Shuffle your schedule

Ask if you can take your lunch break early or late if you need to make job-hunt phone calls. You're much more likely to catch people than if you phone between 1 and 2 p.m. when most people are away from their desks.

Work everywhere

Bring your job-hunting file to work and ask your employer if you can stay a bit late to use the Internet. Soon after going-home time you'll have the place to yourself. You'll be amazed how much you can get done when the place is quiet.

Cut down on TV

It's not 'relaxing' – it's a serious time-sapper. If you're trying to job-hunt at home in the evenings and struggle to switch off the goggle-box, just don't switch it on. Be tough with yourself. If you're serious about job-hunting, you're going to have to make sacrifices – and that might mean *Home and Away*.

Be tough on yourself

Revisit your motivation checklist.

Remind yourself that you don't *have* to do anything. But if you don't, you'll be stuck in that temp job forever. Is that what you want? It's *your* life...

66 Use quiet nights at home to get things done

At the moment I'm temping – mostly five days a week – so it can be hard to find the time to look for jobs. I set aside two or three evenings a week to look for jobs, but I always make sure they're nights when my friends won't be doing anything and there's nothing good on TV. I'm really productive in the time I set aside because I know I'm not missing out on anything. If I didn't spend those evenings job-hunting I'd just be hanging around the house doing nothing anyway, so it makes sense to use the time wisely. Then I can go out on other nights, guilt-free!

Julia Edwards, 22

2:1, European Studies, Durham University

66 If you can afford it, work part-time

I work three days a week as a sales assistant in a clothes shop, so I have the time to apply for jobs and go to interviews on my two days off. It really helps to know that if I don't use that time wisely, I'll have to wait another week before I get the chance to try again.

Daniel Davis, 23

2:1, Modern Language (Spanish) and Business Management, University of Manchester 99

The problem: 'I can't get out of bed'

If you're lucky enough to have parents to support you while you find your first job, so you don't need to work, you're likely to spend much of the day at home alone. Without anyone there to check up on you, you might find yourself staying in bed until lunchtime, which means you're losing a large chunk of the day, every day. Separating yourself from your duvet at the weekend can also be a problem for graduates who are working during the week – but trying to use their time off to job-hunt. When you're getting up at 7 a.m. every weekday to get to the office, of course you don't want to get up at the same time on weekends to job-hunt.

The rescue remedies:

Getting out of your pit is a major problem – and it's not just a matter of laziness (although clearly plain old-fashioned sloth does play a part). If your mornings just aren't happening for you, ask yourself: what are you telling yourself every time you hit that snooze button? Most likely, you've demonised your job-hunt in your head. You've made it into a horrible chore that you're dreading getting stuck into. If this sounds familiar then you need to re-frame. It's much easier to get up and do a task you want to do, than to get up and do a task you *don't* want to do.

Refresh your memory

Revisit your motivation checklist to remind yourself of why you're doing this job-hunt, and that you're doing it for *you*, not for anybody else. If it's all starting to feel like a chore, psychologists recommend reminding yourself that you're doing this because you *want* to, not because you *have* to. You don't have to. You could just stay in that rubbish temp job, or do bar work for the rest of your life. But wouldn't you rather start working towards getting a job that made you feel good about yourself? You might not want to do all the boring bits you have to do in order to get there, but you *do* want to get there. So suck it up and get on with it.

Rehearse mantras

When you're snoozing in bed, tell yourself 'Today is going to be a *good* day...' Make them as cheesy as you like. Hey, whatever works, right?

Don't set your alarm clock for stupidly early

There's no point setting for 7 a.m. – if you know you'll only hit the snooze button until 11 a.m., feeling four hours behind schedule already. If you struggle to get your act together, you might find it better to set a reasonable, do-able time to start work. Say, 10 a.m.? Even if you don't sit down until 10.30, that's still better than 11 – plus you'll be in the right frame of mind and can start your day without feeling guilty about the hours you've already missed.

Try setting three alarm clocks

Place one outside your room so you have to get out of bed to stop it ringing.

Recruit others to help

Ask your dad to knock on the door before he leaves for work, or your mum to phone once she gets to work.

Don't drink too much in the evenings

A night at the pub with your mates after a soul-destroying day of temping or a lonely day at home is one thing – spending every night caning it is another. If you're working, making a habit of turning up with a hangover is not a good look. If you aren't working, the aftermath of last night's boozing will eat into your job-hunt time – and make the time you do spend on it less productive. Come on – you must have some willpower somewhere.... Are you serious about this job thing, or not?

Find out when you work best

If you've never been a morning person, it might not matter that you don't get up before 10 a.m. – as long as you come into your own later on. (See 'Are you a lark or an owl?' in Chapter 9)

Provide an incentive

Treat yourself to nice bath-time goodies, and delicious food for your breakfast. Knowing that a lovely shower and breakfast awaits makes it easier to prise yourself out of your pit.

TOP TIP

If you catch yourself starting to drink for the wrong reasons, take charge of your booze intake and cut back. If you can't cut back, see your GP. Your drinking could be a symptom of depression. For more on this, see later in this chapter.

The problem: 'I'm taking too many breaks'

On an average day, do you spend more time on 'breaks' than you do working? Take longer breaks than you deserve? Ever taken a short break and ended up accidentally watching a whole DVD? At first, taking long breaks feels naughty and fun, but over time, a sneaking suspicion grows that you're not using your time effectively, which can undermine your confidence further and damage your ability to job-hunt effectively. Those three-hour lunch breaks will give you a downright depressing sense that you're nothing but a lazy loser – which is not good.

The rescue remedies:

Few graduates need to be convinced to take breaks – it's been drummed into us that effective working can only be achieved when we have regular stops. The problem is that we go too far the other way – treating ourselves to far too many breaks that are way too long. Basically, we're far too nice to ourselves.

If this is sounding familiar, would I be right in thinking you were a last-minute reviser for every exam you've ever taken? I thought as much. If that's the case, then it's hardly surprising to hear you're struggling to organise your time now. Let's face it, most of us are pretty pathetic at self-discipline, even at the best of times. But when we leave university the conditions are the worst possible. If you're job-hunting at home, you'll find distraction is everywhere: e-mail, DVDs, video games, the Internet, phone, sleep, food, magazines, personal grooming, morning telly, afternoon telly... And some grads would even rather do laundry and housework than knuckle down and get on with their job-hunt. There really is no end to the lengths you'll go to in order to delay just getting on with it. Plus, there's no one chasing you for progress, you have no fixed time frame and no definite, quantifiable goal. No wonder it's just not happening.

Most likely, break-time will always be a weakness for you. But is there anything you can do to improve matters? Absolutely...

Acknowledge the problem
Recognise you have a vulnerability when it comes to breaks. Accept them as a particular danger zone for you, when you're likely to get distracted.

Know that you need to keep your wits about you in order to avoid slipping into bad habits.

Take baby steps

If your discipline is terrible, start by trying to be good for just one day. If you make an unrealistic pact to be good 'from now on...', you're only setting yourself up to fail.

Shift your mind-set

Don't see breaks as a reward – in doing that, you're only demonising your job-hunt, which will make it harder to get back to work later. Instead, think of breaks as a necessity.

Plan your breaks

You should be aiming for a five- to ten-minute stop every hour and a half. Every morning, schedule them into you hour-by-hour planner. You're making a contract with yourself, for yourself. Stick to it.

Raise your break-awareness

Whenever you take a break, do it consciously. Don't just wander into the sitting room and slump in front of the TV. Taking your break at the planned time gives a sense of legitimacy. If it's unplanned, tell yourself, 'right, I'm having a ten minute tea-break now'.

Try a change of scene

Move to somewhere with fewer distractions – and more eyes on you. If you find working at home difficult, you'll probably find you get a lot more done at your local library, coffee shop or an Internet cafe.

Remember your goals

Keep your motivation checklist to hand. When you know you should be getting back to your job-hunt, remind yourself again of what it's all for.

Stick to your five-minute day plan

With no one chasing you for progress, it's the only target you've got – so make sure you use it.

Use breaks well

Computer games and TV might feel like the best rest – because of the sense of escapism – but it's easy to lose track of time. If the weather is fine, the best break is a blast of fresh air – so take a walk to the shops. If it's raining, read a chapter of your book.

Talk to yourself!

If you're alone and still struggling to get off the sofa, say to yourself: 'Right, break-time is over now!' – out loud, in a firm voice. Bonkers? Maybe – but it works.

Don't torture yourself if you slip up

It's good to feel irritated with yourself after an unproductive day – but don't dwell on what a weak-willed loser you are. Instead, channel your frustration with yourself into making sure you have a better day tomorrow.

 TOP TIP

Don't expect to be 100 per cent productive – you never will be. Set reasonable standards and stick to them. Be tough with yourself if you don't reach them. That way you'll have a better day tomorrow.

Why are breaks so hard to control?

Romilla Ready, trainer and co-author of *NLP for Dummies* and *The NLP Workbook for Dummies,* explains why re-framing works:

'If you're having problems keeping control of your time, don't just think it's a question of will-power. Our behaviour could be governed by our deep-rooted dread of the task ahead. The problem is that we demonise work-time (which we associate with pain), and consider break-time a 'treat' (which we associate with pleasure). We inevitably overindulge in break-time, the more desperate we become to avoid the pain. Over time, our destructive thought processes actually teach us to feel positive about breaks – and negative about work. Re-framing both or either activity by giving a different slant to it can help regain the sense of balance. For example, you could try recognising that you do have a choice in carrying out a task or that getting it finished will mean you can move on to something you find more pleasurable. If you want to do the work, you'll have no reason to put it off. And keeping control of your time will be much easier.'

❝ I've learnt to be tough with myself

Job-hunting and filling in application forms is so tedious, if I didn't allow myself a few breaks in the day I'd go crazy. But I know I have to be disciplined about it or I'd never get anything done. I used to switch on the TV, but now when I get bored and fidgety I go for a long run. Exercise really wakes me up – and when I get back to my desk I swear I can feel the extra oxygen pumping round my brain. I stop again and watch *Neighbours* while I have my lunch – but I always switch it off when the credits roll. If I don't, I could still be watching when the kids' TV starts at teatime…

Julia Edwards, 22

2:1, European Studies, Durham University

The problem: 'I'm not tired – I just feel sluggish all day'

Do you have job-hunting days when the blood just never quite gets pumping? When you just can't seem to get fired up? Like you're working at about 50 per cent of your capacity, but just can't seem to push it any higher? Even if it's been a relatively good one, a whole day spent job-hunting alone can leave you feeling strangely flat.

The rescue remedies:

This problem isn't specific to graduate job-hunters – it's a common complaint of anyone who works alone. Many people (particularly extroverts) simply find they need other people around them – that's where they get their energy from. If this is you, there are a lot of things you can do...

Do some exercise

People who have this problem swear that a large chunk of it is physiological – it's simply a case of getting some adrenalin pumping. Instead of flopping round the house, go for a quick run or a workout. Remember, half an hour out of the house isn't a waste of time if doing it doubles your output capacity when you get back.

Have a change the scenery

Moving to a new physical place (say, your local library) can feel like starting afresh. Having a little 'commute' from your home space to your work space gives you a chance to prepare for your day psychologically, as well as being a good bit of exercise.

Stay in touch

Whether it's meeting a job-hunting friend for a coffee, or having a chat with the girl at the supermarket, interacting with other people will help you get fired up.

Take pride in your appearance

If you're working from home, it can be tempting to stay in your PJs all day. After all, they're comfier, and getting dressed is just a waste of time, right? *Stop*. The ritual of washing (hello, energising shower gel), getting dressed (yes, including shoes) and – for girls – even putting on a bit of make-up can all help get you in the right frame of mind for knuckling down and getting on with your day. It turns out there are good reasons why offices don't let employees come to work in their dressing gowns. It's depressing.

The problem: 'I'm working hard – but I'm not seeing any results'

You're managing to find the time to job-hunt, you're busy ticking things off your five minute day plan and you've applied for lots of jobs. So, if you're putting in the time and effort, why aren't you getting more out?

The rescue remedies:

The good news is that you clearly don't have problems with putting the hard graft in. It could be that you need to change your strategy. But first...

Give it a chance

How long have you been working like this for? It can take up to a couple of months to start seeing results with any given job-hunting technique, so stick at it.

Congratulate yourself

Remember all that hard work you've already put in? OK, so it might not *seem* like it's helped you achieve anything, but remember that everything you do contributes towards the ultimate aim of getting that first job, even if it's just to show you what *doesn't* work, so you can move on and try something else! Plus, you never know, some of the people who have already received your CV might be just about to pick up the phone...

Re-assess your strategy

Ask: What's working? What isn't? If nothing is working, is it possible you're using the wrong techniques for the sectors you want to get into? (For example, are you sending off applications 'blind' for media jobs, when you don't have any experience?) Go back to Chapter 6 and see if there's a better way to tackle the problem.

Find fresh ideas

Speak to people you know in the sector you're interested in, and ask them 'What would you do if you were me?' They might have other ideas of approaches you can try.

The problem: 'I start looking at job sites – but then get distracted by the Internet'

Do you put yourself in front of a computer – but then struggle to keep control of what you're actually doing on it?

The rescue remedies:

Two things are happening here – 1) you're forgetting about the task in hand, and 2) you're being lured away by websites that seem like more fun. Happily, there are several things you can do...

Stick to the plan

Make your five minute day plan and your hour-by-hour planner – and follow them properly. If you tend to lose track of time (and therefore hours of your good job-hunting time), set a kitchen timer to go off every hour to punctuate your day.

Work offline

If you're working on your CV or an application form, you probably don't need to have your Internet browser open. So shut it down. If you keep opening it back up, disable your wireless connection, or unplug your Internet cable. Better still, move away from the computer altogether, when you can. If you're working on an application form, print it off, find a pen or pencil, and go to another room or a cafe to work on it. You'll be surprised by how much easier it is to focus on a task when you aren't surrounded by so many distractions.

Tell your friends you won't be online as much as you have been

Cut down on visits to your personal e-mail account or networking profile page to three times a day: morning, lunchtime and evening. It isn't necessary to check in every three minutes. No one expects you to be online all day. Checking your e-mail three times a day is plenty.

Go public

Try working at a computer where other people can see what's on your screen. Try your local library – it's pretty embarrassing to spend all day surfing gossip websites in there. Plus, knowing that you've actually bothered to change location in order to solve this problem should help to focus better on the task in hand.

The problem: 'Every night I get depressed – and every day I fail to get going'

Is your output zero? Are you frustrated with yourself – but things aren't getting any better? Are you getting depressed, feeling hopeless and helpless? Can you feel your confidence evaporating? If you're trapped in a vicious circle of self-loathing, it can feel like there's no way out of it. You just can't see a way to break the cycle.

The rescue remedies:

Congratulations – you've officially hit rock bottom! Getting this low usually only happens to graduates who are job-hunting at home alone all day (even if you're temping, it's hard to let things get this bad). But take heart, there *is* a way to break the cycle. The key is to really feel that nightly dose of frustration and anger and channel it into something productive that you can actually *use*, in order to make tomorrow a better day than today...

Don't be too hard on yourself
You're not a total loser. And you won't be unemployed forever. Having said that...

Don't be too soft on yourself, either
You need to make some big changes. And you need to give yourself a kick up the backside.

Resolve to make changes
This can't continue – and you don't want it to.

Get focussed
Draw up your motivation checklist, if you haven't already. Keep it to hand at all times.

Re-read Chapter 2
Does any of your gloom come from believing something that isn't even true?

Start small
When you decide to make changes, keep your expectations realistic. If you're at rock bottom today, you won't have an amazing day tomorrow. Start by taking baby steps. And I mean tiny. If today was a '1' out of ten, aim for a '2' tomorrow. If you achieve that, aim for a '3' the next day. You

might never make it up to '10' – but if you can hover around the 6/7/8 mark on most days, you'll be doing well.

Get a job

Consider taking on voluntary or part-time work if you aren't already, to keep you in the land of the living.

Find people to talk to

Others in the same boat, who understand what you're going through. But... don't expect anyone to fix your problems for you – or deliver your perfect first job direct to your doorstep. Your job-hunt is *your* responsibility – and yours alone.

Don't expect never to sink this low again.

Hopefully, you won't – but you might. But if you know how to get out of it this time, you'll be able to do it again. Which makes this the very worst things will get. The good news? That the only way is up!

The problem: 'I'm OK researching – but something's stopping me from applying or networking'

You'll happily spend hours online trawling for vacancies or hunting for information – but when it comes to actually applying, or, worse still, picking up the phone to chase up an application, you find yourself stalling...

The rescue remedies:

You're so close – you just need a bit of an extra push and you'll be there! Remember, while the Internet can be great for information-gathering, you're probably going to have to get on the phone (or get out and meet people) if you want to take things to the next level.

A word about clinical depression

Do you have the 'graduation blues' – or is it the real thing? Dr Claire Archdall, psychiatrist at Bristol Royal Infirmary, explains…

'Although we don't know exactly what causes depression, there is evidence to suggest that you might be more vulnerable to it than normal in the months immediately after graduation. The facts are that many people have their first depressive episode in their twenties (the average age is 27), depression is twice as common in women and the risk is higher if you've been unemployed, or felt isolated and low on confidence for a while. A difficult relationship with your parents and a naturally anxious personality can also contribute.

'How do you know if you're depressed? Mild depression looks different from case to case, but typical symptoms can include a loss of interest or pleasure in things you'd normally enjoy, increased tiredness, and having an abnormally (for you) depressed mood that's present for most of the day, almost every day (even on a good day, when things have gone well). Depressed graduates might also feel a loss of confidence, a sense of guilt, recurring thoughts of death or suicide, find it hard to concentrate, trouble sleeping or notice changes in their appetite. If you're worried you have some of these signs or symptoms then visit your GP, who will assess you and recommend treatment if necessary (which may or may not include medication).

'One more thing: if you're feeling down, lay off the booze – drinking might make you feel better in the short-term but long-term it's a depressant so you'll only make things worse. Likewise, steer clear of drugs, which could increase feelings of apathy.'

Revisit your goals

Dig out your motivation checklist to reacquaint yourself with the reasons why you're doing this.

Be tough with yourself

So you're not mad about using the phone... What's the worst that can happen – they tell you to shove off? You can cope with that, surely?

Don't dodge the difficult stuff

Been dreading one particular task? Break it down into smaller mini-tasks and add it to your five-minute day plan. For example, if you have the name of a friend's friend to contact about setting up a meeting, break that down into: 'draft e-mail', 'send e-mail' and 'chase e-mail'.

Pinpoint the time of the day when you feel best physically

Make your phone calls then. Your voice will sound stronger and you'll be more on the ball. (Often, this is after you've taken some exercise and got the blood pumping.)

Don't just rely on e-mail for contact with the outside world

As tempting as it can be to hide behind your inbox, if you want to show you're serious, nothing beats a bit of voice-on-voice.

The problem: 'I've got a family party coming up – what do I tell everyone?'

It's just a festive family get-together/wedding/christening – so why does it feel like you're about to face a firing squad? When you're working on getting your act together, facing the rellies and a raft of family friends can be a waking nightmare. You just know that the first question they're going to ask is: 'So, what are you doing now?' And then they're going to offer you a whole load of irrelevant advice you didn't ask for.

The rescue remedies:

Oh, the horrific irony. How horrendous that graduating should be the time when you feel most at sea – and also the time when you're asked the most questions about your plans. Parents, friends, extended family – everyone seems to have a sudden fascination with what you're going to do next. To you, it's crystal clear you're in a transitional stage of your life and that questions from the floor are not welcome. But that doesn't stop the barrage of enquiries.

Everyone, it seems, is anxious to hear what you're going to 'become'. (Er, they forget that so are you!) Without a plan, you're a sitting duck. 'These events are classic arenas for family one-upmanship,' says Gael Lindenfield, psychotherapist and author of *Assert Yourself*. 'They're also quite natural times for progress updates – but they're happy and frivolous events so conversation is generally upbeat. It's not the moment to impart low-key, serious or downer news.' If you're going into battle, it pays to have a plan, says Gael.

Don't bury your fears
'These events can be really tricky – and pretending they aren't will make things harder for you. Instead, acknowledge that this will probably be a testing day, and be ready for it.'

Prepare some patter
'Be ready for simple, inevitable questions like "What are you up to now?" Keep the tone upbeat – use humour if you like. Practise short, assertive phrases so you're ready for the pushy ones. "Yes, it's pretty hard-going at the moment, but I have a good action plan – how are things with you?" Most people prefer to talk about themselves.'

Don't talk yourself down
'If you handle these events well, it's actually possible to leave feeling *better* about yourself than when you arrived. Use parties to help re-enforce

your self-belief. Just as talking yourself down will make you feel down, hearing yourself talking firmly and confidently about your plans can be enormously beneficial.'

Don't get trashed

'Keep a check on your alcohol intake. Too much could depress your mood on occasions like this.'

Boost your confidence before you go

'Try relaxation or visualisation exercises, which trick your brain and body into feeling as good as you would if things were actually going that well for you.' You could also read through your job-hunt plan. Reminding yourself that you have a strategy will refresh your confidence.

Smarten up

'Making an effort with your appearance has a huge impact on how you feel on the inside.' Not only will you feel better about yourself than if you'd turned up looking like a tramp, but it also sends out a signal that says to people, 'I'm in control – and on the case,' so people won't assume you're on the back-foot.

Search for a fun crowd

'Work the room, spend time with positive and inspiring people. Chatting to them could give you fresh ideas or new contacts to try. Weddings and parties are great for meeting people you wouldn't normally come into contact with.'

Dodge drunken uncles

Ranty advice that's 40 years out of date is not helpful. 'Keep up your sleeve some phrases for fending off unsolicited advice. Try: "You could be right – I'll think about it later. For now I'd just like to have a break and enjoy Christmas."'

Tailor your chat

Remember: people ask questions for all sorts of reasons. 'Sometimes the person is just being nosy, but other times they might genuinely want to know and be trying to be supportive. And don't forget that it's just as likely they couldn't care less about your career plans – they're just making conversation.'

Take time out

'These events can be exhausting – and they can go on for hours. If you get the chance to duck out for a few minutes, take it.'

And if all else fails… Hang out with the under-10s

They're only interested in fireworks and rollercoasters – they couldn't give a monkey's about your career plans.

66 You don't owe anyone an explanation

I was at a family dinner and my dad's cousin who happens to be a university lecturer leaned across the table and said 'Congratulations on your first, Jane! What are you doing now?' After what seemed like an endless silence, I muttered, 'Er, I'm temping actually.' He kindly said, 'Oh well, we all know these things take time,' but I was mortified. Since then, I've wised up. Now when people ask I just smile and say 'It's a work in progress…' and change the subject, sharpish. It needn't be a big deal. It feels like you're being grilled but often people are only asking out of politeness.

Jane Hewitt, 24
1:1, Sports Therapy, University of Bedfordshire

" Forget about what other people think

When I say I'm a Cambridge graduate and working in recruitment, people often seem to think they've misheard me! There are preconceived ideas about 'top' graduates finishing uni and immediately falling into amazing, impressive jobs. But I don't take it personally. The best defence is just to smile, accept that they're responding to a stereotype, and move on. Anyway, I'm really enjoying my job.

Demelza Bowyer, 25

2:1, Modern and Medieval Language, University of Cambridge

Dude, where's my conclusion?

It's customary to finish a book like this with a schmaltzy summing-up about how this is only the beginning of an exceptionally exciting time of your life, and how the yellow brick road that stretches before you is littered with endless possibilities and opportunities. Unfortunately, while I've had a lot of different jobs since I graduated seven years ago, I've never written for a cheesy greetings cards company, so I'm clean out of slush.

That said, there's definitely something in this 'the world is your oyster' business, even if it doesn't seem like it now. But, since I'm well aware that you're a cynical crowd, I know you'll want proof.

I know it's late in the day, but it's time for one last batch of case histories. Like those whose stories feature throughout this book, the people you're about to hear from all graduated without a focussed plan. (And yes, like all the case histories you've read already, they are all 100 per cent real – just look at their weird names if you don't believe me!)

I didn't have to scour the planet to find them – they're all people I know, who are about my age. Some of them are friends I first met at university and some are friends I've met since university, through other friends. Others are people I have met through my work, who have become friends. Apart from being mates of mine, the only thing that makes them different from the people whose stories you read in Chapter 1 is time. These are the grads who finished university a few years before you – and have lived to tell the tale.

You'll see that during the five to 10 years since they graduated, they've made moves that have been brilliant, bonkers and downright bad (it turns out that banana skins can be tricky to spot on the yellow brick road). But they've survived – and picked up bucket-loads of experience, which has helped them make bigger and better decisions about jobs that might be right for them.

The point is that however overwhelming, depressing or impossible things might seem now, flash forward a few years, and you and your friends will have similar stories to tell. I promise.

66 I didn't know then that my job even existed

If you'd told me on my graduation day that I'd end up managing an NHS research centre, I'd have said, 'What's that?' While I had a vague idea of what being a doctor, lawyer or journalist involved, I had no idea that jobs like mine even existed. Before the health service, I worked as a hotel chambermaid, sold advertising space for a trade magazine, and had an admin job for a medical research organisation. I didn't get on the NHS grad scheme first time round either, so I waited a year and reapplied.

Sandra Iskander, 28
2:1, History, Durham University
MSc Health Service Management, University of Birmingham 99

66 I'm juggling jobs – and it's brilliant

I'd never have predicted that seven years after graduating I'd have two jobs – and neither of them permanent. But really, it's OK! I've been juggling IT and stand-up comedy since I graduated – what's changed in that time is my focus. Straight after uni, IT was my day job, and comedy was a sideline. Now that my comedy stuff is taking off (I'm about to take my second show up to the Edinburgh Festival), it's become my main focus and I do freelance IT jobs to top up my income. Who knows what will happen? But I'm really enjoying finding out. It might sound weird but I actually love both jobs. It's fun making people laugh – but I love fixing people's computers too. Strange, but true!

Steve Mould, 29
2:1, Physics, University of Oxford 99

❝ You definitely don't need a 'grand plan'

I've always been into music and I'm very outgoing so perhaps it isn't a huge surprise that I'm now working as a press officer at an independent music PR company. The job is hard work but it's great fun too. I work really closely with all our artists and I go to lots of big industry events like the Brits, the NMEs, and the *Elle* Style Awards. It's not the sort of job you fall into by accident but that doesn't mean I had a 'grand plan' from the start. After uni I worked at Virgin Megastore and HMV, then moved to Sydney where I waited tables and worked in a video shop. Back in the UK, I took a job with a music marketing firm, temped at the BBC and a TV production company, then went back to the same music marketing firm – before landing the job I'm in now. When I look back at my work history, I suppose it's a good thing I'm such a 'people person'. I've certainly met enough of them!

Sam Dowler, 30
2:2, English and Theatre Arts, Goldsmiths College, University of London ❞

❝ Moving around has given me insight

I know it sounds cheesy, but I really love my job. I work for an organisation that encourages the government and businesses to be environmentally conscious in their building projects. I've always been into politics and environmental issues, so after graduation I focussed on a career that would reflect this. Before this job, I worked as a political researcher in Parliament, then in commercial public affairs, and then for the charity WWF. Working for different organisations early in my career gave me a good insight into different parts of the political process.

John Alker, 28
2:1, Geography, University of Oxford ❞

66 My 'big break' came seriously late!

I'm a freelance foreign reporter mainly working for *The Guardian* on social issues, women's issues, and the environment. I've been sent to the Nicaraguan rainforest to interview indigenous tribes about climate change, and Sri Lanka to meet factory workers making cheap clothes sold in UK supermarkets. When I tell people about my work, they assume I've been really focussed but in fact I've had a very disjointed career path – I didn't even get into journalism until I was 25! Fresh out of uni, I worked as a waitress, and then for a digital marketing PR agency. But even after I studied journalism, I moved around a lot, writing for an internet business mag, then for a charity mag, and then co-authoring a book (which bombed). My big break was being offered some temporary 'shift' work on *The Guardian's* 'society' desk. Making contacts there and building my portfolio meant I could sell stories back to the UK press when I later travelled around South America for a year. Now I'm back, I'm thrilled to find I've carved a niche for myself covering stories about social affairs and international development.

Annie Kelly, 31

2:1, English and History, University of Leeds 99

66 I'm freelance and loving it!

I graduated with just the vaguest idea that I wanted to work 'in media'. My first job after uni was as a runner for a TV company, then I worked as a TV scheduler for a broadcasting company. After that, I temped in offices and worked as a lounge pianist at a smart hotel. During that time, I was doing freelance illustrations on the side, and, after 18 months working as the PA to a Mayfair violin dealer, I decided to take the plunge and see if I could get enough work to be a full-time illustrator and cartoonist. Happily, it's going really well. Today I've been designing a set of greetings cards for Marks & Spencer, and I've just finished some work for a charity auction where I painted an enormous guitar for Sir Paul McCartney to sign...

Rosie Brooks, 28

2:2, Music, Durham University

66 I changed my mind – but it's turned out fine!

Like many science grads, I didn't have a clue what to do with my degree when I left university. I did a PGCE and became a secondary school science teacher – but after five years it was time to take stock. Was teaching really for me? As much as I loved some aspects of the job, I just couldn't see myself doing it forever. Re-training as an audiological scientist at 26 was scary – but lots of people start new careers far later than that – some into their forties and fifties! Even though I decided not to stay in teaching, so much of what I learnt has been really useful to me in my current job.

Jane Edgington, 28
1:1, Zoology, Durham University 99

66 I re-trained in my late twenties

My current job as head of 'careers consultancy' at The Careers Group is a zillion miles from my first job when I graduated. Back then, I was passionate about art and wanted to help galleries promote themselves better to the public. My first job after my marketing Masters was as a tour guide at the Glasgow School of Art – after that, I worked as a marketing manager for an architecture and design centre in Glasgow. Then I moved to London to work for Channel 4, arranging events around the UK to run alongside with their summer scheduling. But my best move was taking a job at a recruitment company, which brought me into contact with people considering a career change. To do this full-time I needed to re-train, so I did a Post Grad in Careers Guidance. Since then, I've worked for the University of the Arts in London, Chelsea College of Art and Design, and the London College of Communication.

Susie Goldie, 32
2:1, History of Art, University of Glasgow
Msc Marketing, University of Strathclyde
Postgraduate Diploma in Careers Advice and Guidance, University of East London 99

66 I'm amazed I've become an author!

I never thought I'd be a writer, let alone an author. I didn't write for my uni newspaper, and don't even have English A-level! My post-uni 'career' started with a whimper – I spent the summer temping and learning to type. By October, I was demoralised and desperate for direction so applied on a whim to be office manager at a start-up recruitment company. It was a brilliant first job and my confidence soared – but not for long. When I left to try writing, I was gutted to find that few writing jobs are ever advertised. Knowing I'd need a whole new job-hunt strategy this time, I spent the next four years becoming an expert networker, needling everyone I knew for advice, contacts and references. I took casual work at the *Sunday Express*, *The Sunday Times* and women's magazines *Red*, *NOW*, *Grazia*, *Top Santé* and *Glamour*, until I finally landed my first permanent journalism job as senior writer at *eve*. But I always remembered my directionless days, post uni – and had an idea for a book...

Tanya de Grunwald, 28

2:1, Psychology, Durham University

Useful resources

Here are a few genius websites that should help kick off your job hunt – but remember, it's not an exhaustive list. As you'll soon discover once you get cracking, there are zillions more out there. Happy hunting!

Resources for UK and Ireland

Careers advice and information

The Careers Group: www.careers.lon.ac.uk

C2: www.c2careers.com

GradClub: www.gradclub.co.uk

***The Guardian* Graduate Section**:www.guardian.co.uk/graduate

Prospects: www.prospects.ac.uk

AGCAS: www.agcas.org.uk

Target Jobs: www.targetjobs.co.uk

Recruitments and Employment Confederation: www.rec.uk.com

National Union of Students: www.nusonline.co.uk

The National Council for Work Experience: www.work-experience.org

The British Dyslexia Association: www.bdadyslexia.org.uk

Direct Gov – disabled: www.direct.gov.uk/disabledpeople

EmployAbility: www.employ-ability.org.uk

MIND: www.mind.org.uk

Diversity Now: www.diversitynow.net

Equal Opportunities Commission: www.eoc.org.uk

Vacancy listings

Monster: www.monster.co.uk
Fish4jobs: www.fish4.co.uk/iad/jobs
Workthing: www.workthing.co.uk
Jobcentres: www.jobcentreplus.gov.uk
The Guardian: www.jobs.guardian.co.uk
The Independent: www.jobs.independent.co.uk
The Times: www.timesonline.co.uk/tol/life_and_style/career_and_jobs/
The Telegraph: www.jobs.telegraph.co.uk
The Financial Times: www.ft.com/jobsclassified

Recruitment agencies

Reed: www.reed.co.uk
FreshMinds Talent: www.freshminds.co.uk
Rare Recruitment: www.rarerecruitment.co.uk

Overseas vacancies

Target Jobs: www.targetjobs.co.uk/general-advice/working-in-europe.aspx
Hobsons: www.careersineurope.hobsons.com
Careers in Europe: www.careersineurope.com
EURES: www.europa.eu.int/eures
Overseasjobs.com: www.overseasjobs.com
Japan Exchange and Teaching Programme UK (JET): www.jet-uk.org
British Universities North America Club (BUNAC): www.bunac.org
Gapwork: www.gapwork.com
Voluntary Service Overseas (VSO): www.vso.org.uk
Raleigh International: www.raleigh.org.uk
International Association of Students in Economics and Commerce (AIESEC): www.aiesec.co.uk

Staying motivated

Dude, Where's My Career?: www.careers.lon.ac.uk/dude
Gael Lindenfield: www.gaellindenfield.com
Romilla Ready: www.romillaready.com

Resources for non-UK and Ireland

France

Hobsons: www.hobsons.fr
Target Jobs: www.target-carrieres.fr
ANPE: www.anpe.fr
APEC: www.apec.asso.fr/Accueil/ApecIndexAccueil.jsp

Germany

Staufenbiel: www.staufenbiel.de
Monster: www.monster.de
Stepstone: www.stepstone.de
AZ Online: www.az-online.de

Italy

Mercurius: www.mercurius.it

Norway

Stepstone: www.stepstone.no

Canada

Canadajobs.com: www.canadajobs.com
Globe and Mail: www.globeandmail.com
National Post: www.nationalpost.com
The Star: www.thestar.com

South Africa

Career Junction: www.careerjunction.co.za
Manpower: www.manpower.co.za
Cape Times: www.capetimes.co.za
Independent Online (IOL): www.iol.co.za

Australia

Graduate Careers Australia: www.graduatecareers.com.au
Australian JobSearch: www.jobsearch.gov.au
Positions Vacant: www.positionsvacant.com.au
The Age: www.theage.com.au
The Sydney Morning Herald: www.smh.com.au
MyCareer: www.mycareer.com.au
Recruitment and Consulting Services Association: www.rcsa.com.au

NOTES

NOTES

NOTES

NOTES

NOTES

www.summersdale.com